perfect
jewish

Elizabeth Wolf-Cohen

Bath New York Singapore Hong Kong Cologne Delhi Melbourne

This is a Parragon Publishing book
This edition published in 2008

Parragon Publishing
Queen Street House
4 Queen Street
Bath BA1 1HE, UK

Copyright © Parragon Books Ltd 2004

ISBN 978-1-4075-6350-3

Printed in Indonesia

This book uses imperial, metric, and U.S. cup measurements. Follow the same units of measurement throughout; do not mix imperial and metric. All spoon measurements are level, unless otherwise stated: teaspoons are assumed to be 5 ml, and tablespoons are assumed to be 15 ml. Unless otherwise stated, milk is assumed to be whole, eggs and individual fruit, such as bananas, are medium, and pepper is freshly ground black pepper.

Recipes using raw or very lightly cooked eggs should be avoided by infants, the elderly, pregnant women, convalescents, and anyone with a chronic condition. Pregnant and breast-feeding women are advised to avoid eating peanuts and peanut products.

perfect
jewish

introduction

Jewish cooking is probably one of the most interesting and varied cuisines in the world. Banished from Palestine centuries ago, the Jews had no homeland and so migrated throughout the world, borrowing from local cuisines and using native ingredients. Keeping to kosher requirements and holiday customs, Jews developed dishes suited to the countries and climates where they settled.

Set down in the Bible, the laws of Kashrut pronounced the principles regarding what foods can be eaten and how they should be prepared—"kosher cooking." Some of these principles seem obvious, while others appear arbitrary, but they usually take local traditions into account. Some theorists say that these symbolic rituals were devised to emphasize the Jews' separateness and oneness with God; others find the logic in Scripture. In any case, the strict code required for choosing and preparing food in accordance with health, hygiene, and holiday customs creates a unique Jewish cuisine.

There are two main distinct Jewish groups: the Ashkenazic Jews who mostly came from Central and Eastern Europe and Russia; and the Sephardic Jews from Spain and Portugal, the Middle East, and North Africa. They developed their own cultures and foods in separate geographic areas. Broadly speaking, the dividing line was the mountains separating the North from the South of Europe, from the Caucasus to the Alps and then to the Pyrenees. Significantly, the Jews moved from east to west, not north to south,

encouraging the divisions between the two groups. The differences in their respective cooking styles has to do with climate, soil, and local ingredients. The Ashkenazic world of Northern, Central and Eastern Europe and Russia was a cold, mainly Christian world and Jews were largely provincial, often segregated into ghettoes. Winter vegetables, such as cabbage, carrots, potatoes, and onions, were cooked in chicken and goose fat, while freshwater fish, especially carp and herring, and meat-flavored stews, slowly cooked overnight in bakers' ovens, were favored. The predominant culture was Northern European and Slavic. The Sephardic Jews, by contrast, were mainly Mediterranean and Middle Eastern, living in Islamic cultures. They were more urban, living in cities and ports involved in trade and material pursuits. Their cuisine centered on Mediterranean vegetables, such as bell peppers, eggplant, zucchini, and tomatoes, cooked in olive oil. Saltwater fish, rice, and beans were staples and all dishes were flavored with aromatic herbs and powerful spices. Very rarely did these two different worlds overlap.

ASHKENAZIC

Ashkenazic cooking tends to be subtle and delicate, characterized by lots of well-flavored, slow-cooked beef (and sometimes lamb) stews with onions and garlic. Parsley, dill, and chives are the most frequently used herbs. Horseradish or *chrein* (horseradish-beet) provides a spicy condiment and pickles are the favorite accompaniment.

Eastern European and, especially, Polish combinations of vinegar or lemon juice and sugar or honey add a sweet-and-sour flavor to vegetables and stews. Central European cookery uses goose and chicken fat and smoked or salted fish, as these ingredients were widely available. Potatoes from the New World gained popularity and soon became the base of many traditional Jewish dishes, such as *latkes*, *knishes*, and *kugels*. Barley, lentils, and *kasha* (buckwheat groats) are also common ingredients. Fruit and vegetables are

widely used in Jewish cooking because they are pareve, or neutral, and therefore can be eaten with milk or meat dishes.

Austrian, Hungarian, and German Jews are renowned for their baking. After the second great migration of European Jews to America, many Jews opened bakeries selling breads, bagels, bialys, cakes, yeast cakes, strudels, "Danish," and cookies. These became well-known as Jewish-American foods, but are now very much mainstream.

SEPHARDIC

Sephardic food is light years away from this cold-world cooking; characterized by olive oil, lemons, garlic, aromatic herbs, and sometimes very hot spices. Greek and Turkish Jews use fresh dill, oregano, and coriander, and North African Jews love cumin and dried ginger; cinnamon is widely used in sweet and savory Sephardic dishes. Lamb is the preferred meat in the Sephardic world, as is the saltwater fish of the surrounding seas. Flat and pita breads are eaten throughout the Middle East, Mediterranean, and India, and olives, eggplant, zucchini, tomatoes, bell peppers, and beans are staples. Phyllo pastries with walnuts, almonds, and pistachio nuts, scented with rosewater or orange flowerwater, are more popular than the rich rice puddings and dairy-based sweets of the Ashkenazic world.

Moroccan cuisine, influenced by years of French occupation, is particularly refined and elegant. It combines the foods and flavors of the Sephardic tradition with the technical expertise of French cuisine. Spicy and aromatic, Moroccan cooking uses saffron, preserved lemons (in salt), garlic, fresh coriander, and generous amounts of cinnamon, nutmeg, ginger, and allspice. Yogurt and tahini are used throughout the Middle East and Egypt.

Italian Jews, most of whom lived in the oldest areas of Rome, use many Sephardic traditions in cooking pastas, dumplings, and vegetables. Many of these are referred to as a la Guidea—in the Jewish style.

The Bene Israel Jews, found mostly in Bombay, and the Jews of Cochin in Southern India generally cook in the Sephardic tradition, blending the Indian flavors of cumin, cinnamon, turmeric, coriander, coriander seed,s and cardamom together with chiles and fresh coriander. The arrival of Iraqi Jews in the 19th century added more fresh herbs and greens to the already sophisticated cuisine. Now, the majority of Iraqi Jews live in Los Angeles where they have greatly influenced the style of Californian cuisine.

The founding of the modern state of Israel in 1948 as the Jewish homeland has had a tremendous influence on Jewish cooking. The exciting food revolution led by talented young chefs combining old traditions with new varieties of food has been fueled by the great technological advances in food production, agriculture, and processed kosher foods. Yemenite Jews settling in Israel have added a spicy influence and an individual cuisine. Their cooking includes the use of zhough—a spicy chilli paste—and the making of wonderful breads such as kubaneh.

With the many changes and the movements of peoples and cultures in the Middle East, especially in Israel, Jewish food is continuing to grow and evolve in style and content, respecting its traditions and rituals and creating one of the most exciting, satisfying, and healthy cuisines in the world.

soups, salads & appetizers

Soups, salads, and appetizers are very important in Jewish cooking. The Russian tradition of *zakuski*—a wide selection of hot and cold tidbits—preceded important European meals, for which the *meze*, meaning "table," served the same function in the Middle East. These tasty snacks are what we call "nosh." The line between anosh and an appetizer is a fine one—Chopped Liver (see page 26) on a cracker is "nosh," but attractively garnished on a plate it is an appetizer. These little tidbits are tasty, but they also serve a purpose: the Jews were poor and marginalized, and "noshing" took the edge off the appetite.

Soups were also a way of providing an inexpensive nutritious winter meal. Although chicken soup is probably the most well-known, the majority of Jews love rich, hearty, meat-flavored, or vegetable, soups with lentils, beans, or barley. The Sephardic Jews were fortunate to live in hotter climates and enjoyed "salads" like Hummus (see page 32). Although leafy salads are a more modern addition, they are very popular, as are chopped vegetables such as Israeli Salad (see page 46), now eaten all over Israel.

beet bortsch

serves 6

25 minutes

30–40 minutes

1 lb 8 oz/675 g beets, preferably small tender ones with tops
1 large onion, chopped
15 cups vegetable stock or water
1 tsp salt
pepper

2–3 tbsp freshly squeezed lemon juice
2 tbsp soft light brown sugar, or to taste
chopped fresh dill or snipped chives, to garnish
sour cream, to serve (optional)

There are dozens of Bortsch recipes found throughout Russia, Lithuania, the Ukraine, and other Eastern European countries. It can be made with or without beef and/or additional vegetables added to the essential beets, and served chunky or smooth, hot or cold.

Cut the tops from the beets, leaving a little of the stems attached, and scrub thoroughly under cold running water to remove any grit or sand. Using a swivel-bladed vegetable peeler, peel the beets, then grate. Transfer to a large, heavy pan. (If you like, wear rubber gloves to prevent your hands being stained.)

Add the onion to the pan and cover with the stock. Bring to a boil over medium heat and simmer, partially covered, for 20–30 minutes, or until the vegetables are tender. Remove from the heat and leave the vegetables to cool slightly.

Ladle the liquid into a food processor or blender and process until smooth. Rinse the pan and return the soup to the pan.

Bring to a boil over medium heat and add the salt, pepper to taste, lemon juice, and sugar. Simmer for 2–3 minutes and taste. The soup should have a sweet-and-sour flavor; add a little more lemon juice or sugar if necessary and, if you like, thin with a little more stock.

Serve the soup hot with a swirl of sour cream, if using, and sprinkle with the dill or chives. Alternatively, cool and refrigerate, covered, to serve chilled. (You may wish to thin the soup as it will thicken on chilling.)

cook's tip

If a meat meal is to follow, do not serve the soup with sour cream.

sweet-and-sour
cabbage soup

serves 6

20 minutes

2 hours 30 minutes

2 lb/900 g beef brisket
1 beef soup bone (optional)
8 cups cold water
2 onions, chopped
2 carrots, finely chopped
2 large tomatoes, peeled, seeded, and chopped

1 small cabbage, cored and shredded
1/2 cup seedless raisins
juice of 2 lemons
3–4 tbsp soft light brown sugar, or to taste
salt and pepper

Cabbage was the most commonly used vegetable among the Ashkenazi Jews of Eastern Europe. Boiled, braised, or baked, it was added to potatoes, mushrooms, chestnuts, and carrots and used as a filling for savory pastries and blintzes and, of course, in soup.

cook's tip

To serve as a main course, add 1 lb/450 g peeled, diced potatoes to the soup with the cabbage, then add 2–3 chopped leeks with the cut-up meat. Serve with some crusty bread.

Put the beef, beef bone, if using, and water into a large pan with a tight-fitting lid. Bring to a boil over medium–high heat, skimming any foam that rises to the surface. Boil for 5 minutes, reduce the heat to medium–low and simmer for about 1 hour.

Add the onions, carrots, and tomatoes and a little more water if necessary and continue to simmer for 1 hour, or until the meat is tender. Carefully remove the meat to a cutting board and, if using, remove and discard the beef bone.

Add the cabbage and raisins to the soup and simmer, covered, for 10–15 minutes, or until the cabbage is tender. Add a little more water if the liquid has reduced too much.

Meanwhile, cut the meat into bite-size pieces. Add the meat to the soup and season to taste with the lemon juice, sugar, and salt and pepper. Simmer for 10 minutes more, then taste to check the sweet-and-sour balance. Serve piping hot.

barley &
mushroom soup

serves 8

25 minutes,
plus 20 minutes soaking

1 hour 15 minutes

1 oz/25 g dried wild mushrooms
1 tbsp vegetable oil
1 onion, finely chopped
2 carrots, finely chopped
1 small rutabaga, finely diced
1 lb/450 g fresh mushrooms, chopped

4 cups vegetable stock or water
1¼ cups pearl barley
1 tsp salt
pepper
chopped fresh dill, to garnish

The damp woodlands of Eastern Europe were perfect for wild mushroom picking, especially ceps and chanterelles as they were the most easily identifiable and delicious. They were cooked simply in chicken or goose fat with onions or used to flavor soups and stews.

Put the dried mushrooms into a small heatproof bowl or measuring pitcher and pour over enough boiling water to cover. Leave the mushrooms to soak for 20 minutes.

Heat the oil in a large pan over medium heat. Add the onion and cook for 3–5 minutes, or until softened. Add the carrots, rutabaga, and fresh mushrooms and cook for 5 minutes.

Pour in the stock and bring to a boil over high heat, skimming any foam that rises to the surface. Rinse the pearl barley in a strainer under cold running water and stir into the boiling liquid. Add salt and pepper to taste. Reduce the heat to low and simmer for 30–35 minutes, or until the vegetables and barley are tender, adding more stock if necessary.

Using a slotted spoon, carefully lift the dried mushrooms out of their soaking liquid (do not pour through a strainer or the sand and grit will go into the mushrooms). Slice or chop the mushrooms and add to the soup.

Strain the mushroom liquid through a muslin-lined sieve into the soup. Continue to simmer for 25 minutes, or until the mushrooms are tender, adding more stock if necessary. Serve hot, garnished with dill.

split pea soup
with flanken

serves 8–10

20 minutes,
plus 4–6 hours soaking

2 hours 15 minutes

2 tbsp olive or vegetable oil

2 lb/900 g flanken (see recipe
introduction)

2 onions, finely chopped

2 celery stalks, finely chopped

2 large carrots, finely chopped

1 large potato, finely chopped

2½ cups green or yellow split peas,
soaked for 4–6 hours
or overnight

8 cups beef, chicken or vegetable
stock or water

salt and pepper

chopped fresh parsley, to garnish

Flanken, a bony cut of beef made by cutting across the short ribs, was very important to the Jews of Northern Europe, as were split peas or lentils. Not only were they tasty ingredients, but they supplied the much-needed energy important in those rugged, cold climates.

Heat the oil in a large pan over medium heat. Add the flanken and cook for 5 minutes, or until well colored, turning once. Add the onions and cook for 5 minutes, until softened and just beginning to color. Add the celery, carrots, and potato and cook for 2–3 minutes. Drain the split peas and add to the pan.

Pour in the stock and bring to a boil over high heat, skimming any foam that rises to the surface. Reduce the heat to medium–low and simmer, covered, for 2 hours, or until the meat, vegetables, and split peas are tender, adding a little more stock if necessary and stirring occasionally.

If you like, ladle some of the soup into a food processor or blender and process until smooth. Return to the pan and season to taste with salt and pepper. Serve hot, garnished with parsley.

cook's tip

All you need to serve with this hearty one-pot meal is some dense, dark bread.

variation

Prepare as for Split Pea Soup with Flanken, but omit the flanken and substitute red lentils for the split peas; they do not need soaking, only rinsing. Add 1–2 garlic cloves, 2 ripe peeled, seeded, and chopped tomatoes and ½ teaspoon each of ground cumin, coriander, and cayenne pepper with the other vegetables and finish with a tablespoon each of freshly squeezed lemon juice and extra virgin olive oil.

schav

serves 8

25 minutes,
plus 3–4 hours chilling

6 minutes

1 lb/450 g sorrel, well washed
1 large onion, finely chopped
1 celery stalk, finely chopped
4 cups vegetable stock
    or water
grated zest and juice of 1 lemon
salt and pepper

2–3 tbsp sugar, or
    to taste
sour cream, to serve
fresh dill sprigs, to garnish (optional)

A favorite soup of Eastern European and Russian Jews, schav is a sorrel soup with a slightly sour flavor. Sorrel grows wild in many areas, but it can be difficult to find. Schav is often served at Shavuot, an early summer festival.

cook's tip

If you cannot find sorrel, use young spinach, a bunch of watercress and a little more lemon.

Remove and discard any tough stems from the sorrel and coarsely chop.

Put the sorrel, onion, and celery into a large pan and pour in the stock. Bring to a boil over high heat, skimming any foam that rises to the surface. Reduce the heat and simmer, partially covered, for 20 minutes. Leave to cool slightly.

Ladle the soup into a food processor or blender and process until smooth. Return the soup to the pan and add the lemon zest and juice. Season to taste with salt and pepper and sugar. Pour into a glass bowl and leave to cool. Refrigerate, covered, for 3–4 hours, or until well chilled.

Serve the schav cold in chilled bowls. Spoon in a little sour cream and stir once to swirl. Garnish with a dill sprig, if you like.

italian bean soup
with pasta

serves 6

25 minutes,
plus 8 hours soaking

2 hours

1³/4 cups dried cannellini beans,
    soaked overnight
2 tbsp olive oil
1 onion, finely chopped
1 celery stalk, finely chopped
1 carrot, finely chopped
1 lb/450 g tomatoes, peeled, seeded,
    and chopped
3–4 garlic cloves, crushed

2 bay leaves
2 tsp crushed dried rosemary leaves
1 tsp dried sage
4 cups dried chili flakes
4 cups chicken or vegetable stock
1 cup small dried pasta shapes
3 tbsp each chopped fresh parsley
    and basil, plus extra to garnish
salt and pepper

*Chunky, flavorful bean soups, with
varying seasonings, are popular in
both the Ashkenazic and Sephardic
communities. Although numbers
have now dwindled, Italy was once
home to one of the largest Jewish
communities in the world.*

Drain the soaked beans, rinse, and put into a large pan. Generously cover with cold water. Bring to a boil over high heat, skimming any foam that rises to the surface. Reduce the heat to low and simmer for 1½ hours, or until tender, adding more water as necessary. Remove from the heat.

In a separate large pan, heat the oil over medium heat. Add the onion and cook for 3 minutes, or until beginning to soften. Add the celery and carrot and cook for 4–5 minutes. Add the tomatoes, garlic, bay leaves, rosemary, sage, and chili flakes and cook for 8–10 minutes, or until the vegetables are tender.

Drain the cooked beans, reserving some of the liquid, and add to the vegetable mixture with the stock. Bring to a boil, skimming if necessary.

cook's tip

*If fresh tomatoes are not available,
use canned Italian plum tomatoes.*

Add the pasta to the simmering soup and cook, uncovered, for 8–10 minutes, or until the pasta is tender. Stir in the parsley and basil and season to taste with salt and pepper. Add enough of the reserved bean liquid to make a thick consistency. Serve hot, garnished with extra chopped parsley and basil.

old-fashioned
chicken soup
with matzo balls

serves 8–10

**50 minutes,
plus 8 hours chilling**

3 hours 30 minutes

1 large boiling chicken, weighing
    about 5 lb/2.25 kg, with giblets (no
    liver), neck, and feet, quartered
3 large carrots, cut into pieces
2 large onions, a few skins reserved,
    quartered
2 celery stalks, cut into pieces
2 leeks, split and well rinsed
1 ripe tomato, quartered

2 garlic cloves, peeled
2 chicken stock cubes (optional)
1 tbsp black peppercorns
1 tsp salt
1 bouquet garni
1 quantity Matzo Balls (see
    page 150)
2 tbsp chopped fresh parsley

*Every Jewish community makes
chicken soup and, barring the
variety of seasonings that reflect
their culture, it is very similar.*

Wash the chicken quarters, giblets, neck, and feet and place in a large bowl,
pour over boiling water and drain. Scrape off any skin or grit from the feet.

Transfer to a large pan and cover with cold water. Bring to a boil over high
heat, skimming any foam that rises to the surface. Add the vegetables, stock
cubes, if using, peppercorns, salt, and bouquet garni and continue to boil
and skim for 2 minutes. Reduce the heat to low and simmer for 2½–3
hours, adding more cold water as necessary.

Strain the soup into a large heatproof bowl, reserving the chicken quarters
and giblets. Cool, then refrigerate, covered, overnight. Remove the meat
from the chicken pieces and cut into small pieces. Cut the giblets into small
pieces and add to the chicken. Refrigerate, covered, overnight.

cook's tip

*Instead of Matzo Balls, you
can serve the soup with rice,
noodles, tiny matzo squares,
or Kreplach (see page 158),
which are flour-based dumplings.*

Prepare the Matzo Balls. Carefully scrape off any congealed fat from the
surface of the soup. Transfer to a large pan, add the chicken and giblet
pieces and bring to a boil over high heat.

Drop the Matzo Balls gently into the soup and reduce the heat to
medium. Simmer for 25 minutes, or until the Matzo Balls are puffed and
floating on the surface. Stir in the parsley and serve piping hot.

herrings in sour cream

serves 6–8

20 minutes,
plus 2 hours chilling

1 lb 2 oz/500 g bottled pickled
  herrings or herrings in wine
1 onion, thinly sliced
4 sharp dessert apples, halved and
  cored (not necessary to peel)
2 tsp lemon juice or cider vinegar

½ tsp ground cinnamon
2–3 tsp sugar, or to taste
1 cup sour cream
pepper
pumpernickel bread, to serve

*Herring was an important part of
the Jewish diet in Eastern Europe
because it was the cheapest fish
available. Jews were involved in
importing and selling herrings in
Germany, Poland, and Russia.*

cook's tip

*Most Jewish delis still offer a wide
selection of marinated and pickled
herrings. Be sure to soak salted
herrings in several changes of cold
water for at least 4–6 hours.*

Drain the herrings, discarding the onions and liquid, and pat dry with paper
towels. Cut each herring diagonally into 5 or 6 pieces. Transfer to a non-
metallic mixing bowl and cover with the sliced onion.

Put the apple halves, cut-side down, on the cutting board and thinly slice.
Add to the herrings and onion.

Combine the lemon juice, cinnamon, 2 teaspoons of the sugar and the
sour cream in a small non-metallic bowl. Add pepper to taste, then taste
to check the sweet-and-sour balance. Add a little more sugar if necessary.

Pour the mixture over the herrings, onion, and apples and toss to blend.
Refrigerate, covered, for at least 2 hours or overnight. Serve with
pumpernickel bread.

chopped herring

serves 4–6

20 minutes,
plus 8 hours soaking

12 graham crackers

2 medium cooking apples, or 3–4
Granny Smith apples, peeled,
cored, and cut into quarters

4 large eggs, hard-cooked, shelled,
and quartered

4–6 salted skinless herring fillets,
soaked overnight

3 1/2 tbsp cider vinegar

1/4 tsp ground cinnamon

2 tsp sugar, or to taste

pepper

fresh parsley sprigs, to garnish

*Herring was a staple in the poor
Jewish ghettoes of Eastern Europe,
eaten to break the fast after Yom
Kippur as a way of restoring salt to
the body. Chopped herring is still a
popular appetizer among US,
British, and South African Jews on
the Friday night table.*

Put the crackers into a food processor and process until fine crumbs form.
Pour into a large bowl. Put the apple chunks into the processor and, using
the pulse button, process until chopped; do not over-process or the apples
will be too mushy. Add the apples to the bowl.

Add the eggs to the processor and, using the pulse button, process 4–5
times until chopped; do not over-process. Add the eggs to the bowl. Add
the herrings to the processor and process until chopped; do not over-
process or they will form a paste. Add to the bowl and stir to combine.

Stir in the vinegar, cinnamon, and sugar and add pepper to taste. Taste the
mixture to check the sweet-and-sour balance. Spread the mixture on a flat
serving dish, then refrigerate, covered, until ready to serve. Garnish with
parsley sprigs.

chopped liver

serves 6–8

20 minutes,
plus 2–3 hours 30 minutes
cooling & chilling

20 minutes

1 lb/450 g chicken livers

salt and pepper

2 tbsp chicken-flavored vegetable fat
or vegetable oil, plus extra
if necessary

2 medium onions, finely chopped

3–4 large eggs, hard-cooked, shelled,
and coarsely chopped

chicken or vegetable stock or water
(optional)

fresh parsley or dill sprigs, to garnish

Challah (see page 222), rye bread, or
matzos, to serve

*No-one really knows the origin, but
chopped liver is one of the best-
known and best-loved Jewish foods.
Although there are few ingredients,
the taste and texture vary from
country to country. It is usually
made with chicken livers.*

To make kosher: preheat the broiler to medium heat. Wash the livers in
cold water, drain, and pat dry with paper towels. Sprinkle with salt to taste.
Arrange the livers on a rack over a foil-lined baking sheet. Broil gently for
4 minutes, or until the surface looks dry and lightly colored. Turn and broil
the other side for 3–4 minutes, or until just cooked through; the livers
should have no pink remaining. (The purpose of koshering is to remove
any traces of blood.) Allow the livers to cool and drain.

Meanwhile, heat the fat or oil in a heavy-bottom skillet over medium heat.
Add the onions and cook for 10 minutes, or until soft and golden, stirring
occasionally.

Put the livers into a food processor with the onions and process until just
blended. Add the eggs and season to taste with salt and pepper. Process
until blended, but not pasty; if the mixture seems dry, add a little more fat
or oil, or a little stock or water.

Spoon into a serving bowl or mold rinsed with a little cold water,
smoothing the top. Refrigerate, covered, for 2–3 hours, or until ready to
serve. Spread or scoop on to small plates and garnish with parsley or dill
sprigs. (To unmold, dip the mold into hot water and invert on to a serving
plate.) Serve with Challah, rye bread, or matzos.

falafel

makes about 30 balls

30 minutes

15 minutes

1 lb 12 oz/800 g canned chickpeas
1 slice day-old bread, crust removed
1 onion, quartered
4 garlic cloves, or to taste, peeled
2 tbsp chopped cilantro or parsley
1 tbsp ground coriander
1 tbsp ground cumin
1–2 tsp salt

1/4–1/2 tsp cayenne pepper
pepper
3 tbsp all-purpose flour or bulgur
   wheat
1 tsp baking powder
vegetable oil, for frying
pita bread, salad, hot pickles, and
   tahini, to serve

These tasty deep-fried snacks are eaten all over the Middle East, but in Israel they are almost a national treasure. They can be eaten on their own or as part of a meze or in a warm pita with salad and tomatoes and a drizzle of tahini or Zhoug (see page 138).

Drain and rinse the chickpeas, reserving about 3–4 tablespoons of the liquid, and dry well. Drizzle 1 tablespoon of the reserved liquid over the bread slice and allow to soak in, then squeeze dry. Put the bread and chickpeas into a food processor and process until a soft paste forms; you may need to work in batches. Transfer the mixture to a large bowl.

Put the onion into the processor, process until finely chopped and add to the chickpea mixture. Process the garlic and cilantro until finely chopped and add to the chickpea mixture. Add the ground coriander, cumin, salt, and cayenne pepper to the mixture and season to taste with pepper. Stir to combine.

Sprinkle over the flour and baking powder. Using your hands, mix until a soft dough forms, adding more of the reserved liquid to bind if necessary. Using wet hands, shape the mixture into walnut-size balls and set them on a baking sheet. Falafel can be prepared ahead to this point, then refrigerated until time to cook.

Heat about 3 inches/7.5 cm of vegetable oil in a deep-fat fryer or wok to 350–375°F/180–190°C, or until a cube of bread browns in 30 seconds. Working in small batches, slide the balls into the oil and cook for 2–3 minutes, or until a rich golden-brown color, turning to color evenly. Using a slotted spoon, transfer to paper towels to drain. Serve warm in pita bread with salad, hot pickles, and tahini.

eggplant dip

serves 8–10

15 minutes,
plus 2 hours chilling

35 minutes

2 medium eggplants, weighing about
 1 lb 9 oz/700 g

3–4 tbsp freshly squeezed lemon
 juice, or to taste

3½ tbsp tahini

3–4 garlic cloves, crushed

salt and pepper

2–3 tbsp extra virgin olive oil, plus
 extra for drizzling

to garnish
chopped fresh parsley
a few black olives
warm pita bread or matzos, to serve

There are many versions of this delicious smoky eggplant and tahini dip all over the Middle East. It is sometimes called eggplant caviar or baba ghanoush.

cook's tip

This dip is excellent made from eggplants cooked over barbecue coals for 30–40 minutes, or until the skins are charred and shriveled and the flesh is meltingly tender.

Preheat the oven to 450°F/230°C. Pierce the eggplants all over with a sharp knife and place on a baking sheet. Bake for 35 minutes, or until tender and collapsed, turning frequently. Leave to cool slightly.

Cut each eggplant in half lengthwise and scoop out the flesh into a food processor. Process until smooth.

Add the lemon juice, tahini, and garlic and season to taste with salt and pepper. Process until blended. With the machine running, slowly add the oil until the dip is well blended and creamy. Adjust the seasoning, if necessary, and spoon into a bowl. Refrigerate, covered, for at least 2 hours or overnight.

To serve, spoon into a shallow dish or on to individual plates and, using a spoon, make a shallow well in the center. Drizzle over a little extra oil and sprinkle with parsley and olives. Serve with warm pita bread or, at Passover, matzos.

hummus

serves 8–10

20 minutes

1 lb 12 oz/800 g canned chickpeas
3–4 garlic cloves, finely chopped
3½ tbsp freshly squeezed
  lemon juice
3½ tbsp tahini, plus extra for serving
  (optional)

salt
cayenne pepper
chopped fresh parsley, to garnish
olive oil (optional) and hot toasted
  pita bread, to serve

This delicious creamy dip, an ancient specialty of Middle Eastern Jews, has become so popular that it is sold all over the world in supermarkets and delis. In Jerusalem, it is served drizzled with olive oil, then sprinkled with paprika and pine nuts.

Drain and rinse the chickpeas, then drain again thoroughly. Reserve 2 tablespoons of the chickpeas to garnish. Put the remaining chickpeas in a food processor with the garlic and process to blend.

Add the lemon juice, tahini, and 1–2 tablespoons of water and process until smooth. Season to taste with salt and cayenne pepper. Transfer to a non-metallic bowl and stir in a little more water to form a smooth, creamy, thick sauce. Refrigerate, covered, for up to 5 days.

To serve, spread the hummus in a thin layer (about ¼ inch/5 mm thick) on a plate or shallow bowl. Using the back of a spoon, make a hollow in the center and, if you like, pour in a little oil or extra tahini. Chop the reserved chickpeas and sprinkle over, then dust with cayenne pepper and sprinkle with parsley. Serve with toasted pita bread.

jewish-style artichokes

serves 6

25 minutes

25 minutes

2–3 lemons, cut in half
12 small young Italian-style
    artichokes
olive oil
1 bunch fresh flat-leaf parsley, finely
    chopped
1 small bunch fresh basil leaves, torn
    into pieces

4–5 garlic cloves, finely chopped
1 tsp salt
pepper
2 cups matzo meal, for coating
fresh parsley or basil leaves,
    to garnish

This famous dish was introduced to Rome by Jews during the Middle Ages. It was originally made with special tiny local artichokes, which were trimmed and soaked, fanned out and fried in oil until they resembled sunflowers.

cook's tip

Look for the small, long, purplish artichokes found in specialist Italian shops and markets. Although larger globe artichokes can be used, they need careful trimming and the outer leaves and hairy choke must be removed.

Half fill a large bowl with water and squeeze in the lemon juice from the lemons. Add the lemon halves to the water.

Remove any tough or broken outer leaves from the artichokes and trim the tops with a sharp knife. Cut the stems to 2–3 inches/5–7.5 cm long and peel the remaining stem, if necessary. Put each artichoke into the lemon water as you prepare them; this prevents discoloration.

Combine ½ cup of oil with the parsley, basil, garlic, and salt and pepper to taste in a small bowl. Pour the matzo meal into a shallow dish and set aside.

Drain the artichokes. Holding each artichoke by its stem, press the top flat against the work surface to spread open the leaves. Spoon in some of the olive oil dressing between the leaves, then roll each one in the matzo meal to coat evenly.

Heat about ¼ inch/5 mm of oil in a large, heavy-bottom pan over medium heat. Arrange the artichokes in the pan in a single layer and cook, covered, for 25 minutes, or until tender and golden-brown, turning 3–4 times to brown evenly. Transfer to a serving plate and spoon over any pan juices or drizzle with fresh oil and leave to cool to room temperature before serving. Garnish with parsley or basil.

south american
pickled fish

serves 4–6

40 minutes, plus
2–3 hours chilling

2 lb 4 oz/1 kg mixed firm white fish
   fillets, such as sole, red snapper,
   and halibut (skinless, if you prefer)
1 cup freshly squeezed lemon juice
1 cup freshly squeezed lime juice
2 fresh red chiles, thinly sliced

2 red onions, thinly sliced
2 garlic cloves, finely chopped
pinch of sugar
salt and pepper
cilantro leaves, to garnish

As Jews emigrated to various countries, they incorporated local ingredients and local customs into their culinary repertoire. Known as ceviche, this dish is popular with Jews in Mexico and South America. Jews have pickled fish in many ways for centuries.

Cut the fish diagonally into 1-inch/2.5-cm strips and arrange them in a large non-metallic dish.

Combine the lemon and lime juices, chiles, onions, garlic, and sugar in a non-metallic bowl. Season to taste with salt and pepper. Pour over the fish strips, spreading evenly over the fish.

Refrigerate, covered, for 2–3 hours, or until the fish strips turn white and opaque. Do not marinate any longer than 3 hours or the fish will begin to disintegrate as the acids continue to break down the proteins.

Arrange some strips of each kind of fish on plates and spoon over some of the dressing, being sure to distribute the chiles and onions evenly. Garnish with cilantro leaves and serve.

piroshki

makes about 36 pastries

30 minutes, plus
2 hours 20–30 minutes chilling

25–55 minutes

I lb/450 g good-quality store-bought
  puff or plain pastry

filling

I tbsp vegetable oil
I onion, finely chopped
I cup ground beef or veal,
  or a combination of both

I tsp salt
pepper
freshly grated nutmeg, to taste
¼ tsp dried thyme
2 tbsp finely chopped fresh parsley
2 eggs, beaten

*Russian Jews who emigrated to
America popularized these little
filled pastries. This version uses a
good-quality, store-bought pastry
and ground beef for the filling.
Serve with Chicken Soup
(see page 20) or Bortsch
(see page 8), or as a
snack or appetizer.*

Prepare the filling. Heat the oil in a medium skillet over medium heat. Add
the onion and cook for 5 minutes, or until soft and beginning to color. Add
the meat and cook for 5–8 minutes, or until no pink remains and any liquid
has evaporated, stirring occasionally. Add the salt and pepper and nutmeg
to taste. Stir in the herbs. Remove from the heat and mix in half the beaten
egg. Spoon into a bowl, leave to cool, then refrigerate, covered, for at least
2 hours or overnight.

Preheat the oven to 400°F/200°C. Lightly grease 2 large baking sheets
(you may need to bake the piroshki in batches). Divide the pastry into
quarters and work with one piece at a time. On a lightly floured work
surface, roll out the dough to about ⅛ inch/3 mm thick.

Using a 3-inch/7.5-cm round cutter, cut out as many circles as possible.
Brush the edge of each circle with a little of the beaten egg and place a
rounded teaspoon of filling on the circle. Fold one side over to form a half-
moon shape and press the edges together to seal. Use a kitchen fork to
press a decorative edge on to the sealed edge. Re-roll any dough scraps
and continue forming the piroshki with the remaining dough and filling.

Arrange the piroshki on the baking sheets about 2 inches/5 cm apart and
refrigerate for 20–30 minutes. (Refrigerate any others that do not fit on
the baking sheets until the baking sheets can be re-used.)

Brush the top of each piroshki with beaten egg. Bake for 15–20 minutes,
or until puffed and golden. Remove to a wire rack to cool slightly.

potato knishes

makes about 24 pastries

30 minutes, plus
2 hours 30 minutes chilling

1 hours 15 minutes

pastry
2½ cups all-purpose flour, sifted
1 tsp baking powder
½ tsp salt
4 oz/115 g unsalted butter or hard
    margarine, cut into small pieces
about ½ cup soured cream
1 egg, beaten, for glazing

filling
2 tbsp butter or oil
2 onions, finely chopped
2–3 large potatoes, cooked, drained
    and mashed
1 egg
salt and pepper

Originally sold from handcarts at the turn of the 19th century by Russian and Eastern European Jews, knishes are now big business and are still king of street food in New York. A cottage cheese filling is traditional at the early summer agricultural festival of Shavuot.

Prepare the pastry. Put the flour, baking powder, and salt into a food processor and pulse to blend. Add the butter and process until fine crumbs form. Spoon the sour cream over the mixture and process until a dough begins to form; do not allow the dough to form a ball or the pastry will be tough. If too dry, add a little water at a time and pulse.

Turn out on to a lightly floured work surface and knead lightly. Form into a ball and flatten to a disk shape. Wrap and refrigerate for at least 2 hours.

Prepare the filling. Heat the butter in a skillet over medium heat. Add the onions and cook for 15 minutes, or until soft and golden, stirring frequently. Remove from the heat, stir in the potatoes and cool slightly. Beat in the egg and salt and pepper to taste. Leave to cool completely.

On a lightly floured work surface, roll out the dough to about ⅛ inch/3 mm thick. Cut the dough into 4-inch/10-cm squares and place a tablespoon of filling in the center of each. Brush the edges with a little beaten egg and fold the lower left-hand corner up to the upper right-hand corner to form a triangle. Press to seal well, then use a fork to press a decorative edge on to the sealed edge. Re-roll any dough scraps and continue forming triangles with the remaining dough and filling. Refrigerate on trays for 30 minutes. Preheat the oven to 400°F/200°C.

Arrange the triangles 1 inch/2.5 cm apart on 2 large nonstick baking sheets. Brush with beaten egg. Pierce the top of each. Bake in batches for 20 minutes, or until puffed and dark golden brown. Cool on a wire rack.

egg & onion

serves 6

15 minutes

1 large onion, quartered

8 large eggs, hard-cooked, shelled, and quartered

2–3 tbsp chicken fat, soft margarine, or chicken-flavored vegetable fat

salt and pepper

strained hard-cooked egg yolk and sliced scallions, to garnish

rye or black bread, to serve (optional)

This egg dish is often served as an appetizer alone or with Chopped Liver (see page 26) for a Friday night dinner. Use cooked onions or scallions for a milder flavor.

cook's tip

Serve with slices or thin strips of smoked salmon for extra elegance.

Put the onion quarters into a food processor and, using the pulse button, process until finely chopped, but not mushy.

Add the egg quarters and the chicken fat and, using the pulse button, process until just blended; do not over process as the texture should not be too smooth. Season to taste with salt and pepper.

Spoon into a serving bowl or plate and refrigerate, covered, until ready to serve. Spoon or scoop on to plates and garnish with a little hard-cooked egg yolk pushed through a strainer with the back of a spoon and sliced scallions. Serve with slices of rye or black bread, if you like.

gefilte fish

serves 6–8

45 minutes, plus
3–4 hours 30 minutes chilling

1 hour 30 minutes

stock

3 lb/1.3 kg white fish bones and
heads, well rinsed

2 onions, sliced

2 carrots, sliced

1 celery stalk, sliced

4–5 fresh parsley sprigs

1 tsp salt

1 tsp black peppercorns

1 tsp sugar

filling

4 lb/1.8 kg mixed skinless white fish
fillets, such as cod, halibut, and
snapper, together with a little carp
or pike, cut into pieces

2 onions, coarsely chopped

3 eggs, lightly beaten

1 1/2–2 tsp salt

1/2 tsp ground white pepper

1/4 tsp freshly grated nutmeg

1/2 cup matzo meal

3 1/2 tbsp water

1 carrot, thinly sliced

fresh parsley sprigs and lemon
wedges, to garnish

Chrein (see page 130),
to serve

*As long ago as the Middle Ages,
German Jewish housewives
chopped and stuffed pike to serve
on the Sabbath. Nowadays, gefilte
fish is usually a combination of
chopped white fish seasoned and
formed into "quenelle"-shaped
dumplings, poached in fish stock.*

Put the stock ingredients into a large pan, cover with water and bring to a
boil over high heat, skimming any foam that rises to the surface. Reduce
the heat and simmer for 30 minutes. Strain into a large pan.

Prepare the filling. Put the fish and onions into a food processor and
process to a fine paste; you may need to work in batches. Add the eggs,
salt, pepper, and nutmeg and process to blend. Scrape into a large bowl.
Stir in the matzo meal and water, a little at a time; the mixture should be
slightly sticky, but hold its shape. Refrigerate, covered, for 30 minutes.

Form the mixture into ovals using 2 tablespoons and set on a dampened
baking sheet. Return the stock to a boil. Carefully lower the ovals into the
stock. Reduce the heat and simmer gently for 1 hour. Add the carrot after
30 minutes. Remove from the heat and leave to cool.

Remove the ovals to a serving dish. Strain over the stock. Place a carrot
slice on top of each oval. Scatter over the remaining slices. Refrigerate,
covered, for 3–4 hours or overnight. Garnish and serve with the sauce.

israeli salad

serves 4

20 minutes

2 large ripe tomatoes
1 large cucumber, peeled
1 green bell pepper, seeded
1 large red onion or 1 bunch scallions

$^1\!/_2$ bunch fresh parsley
3–4 tbsp extra virgin olive oil
juice of 1 lemon
salt and pepper

This salad is an Israeli classic. Originally it was part of the breakfast "buffet" on the Kibbutzim, with the ingredients laid out like a salad bar and everyone making their own combinations. The vegetables should be cut into dice about $^1\!/_4$ inch/5 mm square.

Core the tomatoes and slice, then chop into very small dice. Transfer to a large salad bowl. Quarter the cucumber (scrape out the seeds, if you like) and dice into very small pieces. Add to the salad bowl. Dice the green bell pepper and add to the other salad vegetables. Chop the onion very finely and add to the bowl.

Strip the leaves from the parsley stems and chop. Add to the salad bowl and toss with the salad vegetables.

Combine the oil, lemon juice, and salt and pepper to taste in a small non-metallic bowl. Taste to check the seasoning, then pour over the salad vegetables and toss well to coat. Serve immediately.

variation

Serve the above vegetables with a tahini dressing: stir together 3–4 tablespoons of tahini with 2 tablespoons, or to taste, of freshly squeezed lemon juice in a small non-metallic bowl. Season to taste with salt and pepper. Thin the dressing with a little water and more lemon juice to a coating consistency.

moroccan grated
carrot salad

serves 4–6

15 minutes,
plus 3–4 hours chilling

5 minutes

1 lb/450 g carrots, peeled (and lightly cooked, if you prefer)

3–4 tbsp extra virgin olive oil or vegetable oil

2 garlic cloves, chopped

1 tsp salt

1½ tsp ground cumin (optional)

½ tsp crushed dried red chili flakes

1 tsp sugar

2–3 tbsp chopped cilantro or parsley, plus a few leaves to garnish

3–4 tbsp freshly squeezed lemon juice

This slightly sweet and spicy salad is popular in Israel and all over the Middle East. Some traditionalists prefer to cook the carrots lightly before grating, but raw carrots add freshness and color.

variation

Add the juice and grated rind of 1 orange and ¼ teaspoon of ground cloves to the dressing.

Using a hand grater or a food processor fitted with a grater blade, grate the carrots and turn into a large bowl.

Heat 2 tablespoons of the oil in a small skillet over medium heat, add the garlic and fry for 2 minutes, or until the garlic begins to color. Add the salt, cumin, if using, chili flakes and sugar, stirring to blend. Remove from the heat and leave to cool slightly.

Stir in the remaining oil, chopped cilantro and lemon juice. Pour over the carrots and toss well to blend.

Cover and refrigerate for 3–4 hours or overnight. Spoon into a serving bowl and garnish with the herb leaves.

beet & watercress salad
with mustard vinaigrette

serves 6

20 minutes

1–2 large bunches watercress, well rinsed and trimmed

10–12 small cooked beetroot, peeled and diced

mustard vinaigrette

2 fl oz/50 ml white wine vinegar

1/2 tsp sugar (optional)

2 garlic cloves, crushed

1 tbsp Dijon mustard

salt and pepper

5 tbsp vegetable oil

5–6 tbsp olive oil

Beets have been a staple in the Russian-Jewish community for centuries. Pickled beets brought color and sharpness to an otherwise bland diet and cold beet salads were plentiful. This is a lively sweet-tangy salad.

variation

For the typical Sephardic beet salad, toss the beets, diced or sliced, with a little olive oil, lemon juice, and salt and pepper to taste. Garnish with fresh parsley or cilantro.

Prepare the vinaigrette. Whisk together the vinegar, sugar, if using, garlic, mustard, and salt and pepper to taste in a small bowl until well blended.

Using a whisk or kitchen fork, slowly whisk in the vegetable oil, a little at a time, until smooth, then whisk in the olive oil, until a creamy dressing forms. Taste to check the seasoning and set aside.

Put the watercress into a large bowl and drizzle over a little of the dressing. Toss to coat the leaves lightly, and arrange on individual plates, reserving a few watercress leaves. Put the beets into a separate bowl. Add the remaining vinaigrette (or to your taste) and toss to combine.

Spoon the beet mixture into the center of the watercress leaves and garnish with the reserved watercress leaves. Serve immediately.

hot potato salad

serves 4–6

20 minutes

25 minutes

2 lb 4 oz/1 kg waxy potatoes
2 German-style dill pickles, diced
3½ tbsp wine vinegar (red or white)
2 tbsp vegetable oil, plus extra for
 drizzling (optional)
1 onion, finely chopped
1–2 garlic cloves, finely chopped

1 celery stalk, finely chopped
salt and pepper
1 tbsp soft light brown sugar
1 tbsp German mustard
1–2 tbsp chopped fresh parsley

Since the 18th century, when Frederick the Great gave away free seed potatoes to the poor to help stave off famine, potatoes have been an integral part of the Jewish diet. In Germany, potatoes were used in bread, soup, pancakes, and dumplings as well as in salads.

Peel the potatoes and cut into ½-inch/1-cm cubes. Bring a large pan of salted water to a boil over high heat. Add the potato cubes and return to a boil. Simmer for 10 minutes, or until just tender, then drain. Do not over-cook.

Turn the potatoes into a large mixing bowl and add the pickles and sprinkle with half the vinegar. Toss lightly.

Heat the oil in a skillet over medium heat. Add the onion and cook for 2–3 minutes, or until just beginning to soften. Add the garlic and celery and cook for 2–3 minutes, stirring frequently. Season to taste with salt and pepper, then stir in the sugar, mustard, and remaining vinegar until the mixture is well blended.

Pour the mixture over the potatoes in the bowl, add the parsley and toss gently to mix. Spoon into a serving bowl and serve warm. If you like, drizzle with a little more oil.

orange, avocado &
mint salad with pomegranate seeds

serves 4

30 minutes

1 seedless orange
1 ripe pomegranate, divided
 into sections
2 ripe avocados
freshly squeezed juice of ½ lemon
4 tbsp white wine vinegar
1–2 tbsp honey

salt and pepper
2 tbsp extra virgin olive oil
1 tbsp sunflower oil
½ bunch fresh mint, leaves stripped
 from stems
about 24 Kalamata olives, stoned

*The avocado is one of Israel's top
exports and is used in may ways:
in salads and appetizers, even as
baby's first fruit! Shamouti oranges
are also an export fruit, as are
pomegranates. This salad is a
perfect way to combine them.*

With a very sharp knife, carefully peel the skin from the orange, removing
all the white pith. Over a bowl, remove the orange sections by sliding the
knife between the membranes, Allow the sections to drop into the bowl.
Squeeze the remaining membranes, adding the juice to the bowl. Using a
teaspoon, scrape out the pomegranate seeds into a separate small bowl,
discarding any pieces of white membrane. Squeeze the juice from the
pomegranate sections into another small bowl.

Cut the avocados in half and remove the stones. Run a round-bladed knife
between the skin and flesh, separating the flesh from the skin.

Invert the avocados on to a board. Remove the skin. Cut lengthwise slices
into the avocados, leaving them joined at the stalk end. Set each half on a
salad plate. Using the palm of your hand, gently press the slices forward to
fan out. Sprinkle with lemon juice.

Whisk together the vinegar, honey, and salt and pepper to taste in a small
bowl. Add about 2 tablespoons of the orange juice and 1 tablespoon of
the pomegranate juice. Whisk in the oils and half the mint leaves.

Divide the orange segments and olives between the salad plates, sprinkle
with the pomegranate seeds and drizzle over the dressing. Garnish with
the remaining mint leaves. Serve immediately.

home-made pickled cucumber
salad with dill

serves 6–8

15 minutes, plus 8 hours chilling

1 large cucumber
4 tbsp white wine or cider vinegar
1–2 tbsp sugar, or to taste
2–4 tbsp finely chopped fresh dill
½ cup water
salt and pepper

Cucumber salads are prepared in many ways in both the Ashkenazic and Sephardic communities. The Ashkenazi preference is for a sweet-and-sharp vinegar-based marinade, while the Sephardi taste is for a yogurt base.

Using a swivel-bladed vegetable peeler, lightly peel the cucumber in alternate stripes. Using a food processor fitted with a slicing disk, thinly slice the cucumber and turn into a large bowl with the juices.

Combine the vinegar, sugar, dill, water, and salt and pepper to taste in a small bowl. Pour over the cucumber and refrigerate, covered, overnight. Serve chilled.

For a Sephardic version
Omit the vinegar marinade and combine 1 cup natural yogurt, 1 crushed garlic clove, 2 tablespoons lemon juice, 3–4 tablespoons chopped fresh mint or dill, and salt and pepper to taste. Pour over the cucumber. Refrigerate overnight and serve chilled.

tabbouleh

 serves 10–12

 20 minutes,
plus 8 hours soaking

generous 1 cup cracked wheat or bulgur wheat

2 large ripe tomatoes, peeled, seeded, and chopped, or 4–5 canned Italian plum tomatoes, finely chopped (liquid reserved)

1 cucumber, peeled, seeded, and finely chopped

1 red onion, or 4–6 scallions, finely sliced

1/2 bunch fresh parsley, chopped

1 small bunch fresh mint, finely chopped

juice of 2–3 lemons

3/4 cup extra virgin olive oil, plus extra for serving (optional)

salt and pepper

fresh mint leaves and Kalamata olives, to garnish (optional)

In many Sephardic communities, cracked or bulgur wheat is used as an alternative to rice, especially as an accompaniment or stuffing for poultry. Here, it features in this well-known Middle Eastern salad.

Put the cracked wheat into a large bowl, add enough cold water to cover and leave to soak for 8 hours, or overnight, until puffed and tender, stirring occasionally. Add more water if necessary.

Turn into a strainer to drain any excess liquid, then turn on to a clean dish towel, roll up, and gently squeeze dry. Transfer to a large bowl and fluff up lightly with a fork.

Add the tomatoes, cucumber, onion, parsley, and mint and toss until combined. Stir in the lemon juice and oil, and season to taste with salt and pepper; the flavor should be tangy and herby. Refrigerate, covered, until ready to serve.

Spoon the tabbouleh on to a shallow serving dish. Sprinkle with mint leaves, a few Kalamata olives and drizzle with a little more oil, if you like.

main dishes

Historically, the Jews were basically vegetarian. Most people could not afford meat and, of course, storage and spoilage were important health issues. Meat, poultry, and fish dishes were a tradition reserved for celebrating the Sabbath or holidays. Many traditional meat dishes are slow cooked and rely on a small amount of meat or bones to flavor a casserole of beans and vegetables. Because of the prohibitions of the dietary laws (Kashrut) limiting the hanging of meat to tenderize it, slow cooking was a practical alternative.

In general, Ashkenazic Jews prefer beef because lamb and mutton were not available in Eastern Europe. However, in the Sephardic communities of the Middle East and North Africa, lamb was more readily available and preferred. Although poultry is popular among all Jews today, traditionally goose was the most important meat in Central and Eastern Europe, where their rearing was a Jewish occupation. Chicken was symbolic of several rituals within Sephardic communities and was often more expensive than meat, so many of their chicken recipes are for festive occasions. Fish is a popular choice for all Jews because it is *pareve*, or neutral, and can therefore fit into meat and dairy meals alike.

roast chicken
with herby matzo stuffing

serves 4–6

20 minutes, plus
30 minutes standing & Resting

I hour 45 minutes

I roasting chicken, weighing
3 1/2–4 lb/1.6–1.8 kg, rinsed
and dried
I lemon, cut in half
salt and pepper
I tbsp chicken fat or vegetable oil
I onion, quartered
1/2–I cup water
fresh parsley, to garnish

matzo stuffing

2–3 matzos, broken into small pieces
1/2 cup chicken soup, stock, or water,
heated
2 tbsp chicken fat or vegetable oil
I large onion, finely chopped
I celery stalk, finely chopped
3–4 tbsp chopped mixed fresh herbs
I egg, lightly beaten

*Poultry has been a staple of Jewish
cooking since the Middle Ages, its
popularity partly due to the fact
that, according to the Kashrut
(kosher laws), slaughtering was
possible without a shochet
(professional slaughterer).*

Preheat the oven to 400°F/200°C. Prepare the stuffing. Put the matzos
into a large bowl and pour over the soup. Leave to stand until absorbed.
Heat the fat in a skillet over medium heat, add the onion and celery and
cook for 5 minutes, or until soft and golden. Cool slightly and stir into the
matzo mixture. Cool, then stir in the herbs and egg.

Rub the outside of the chicken with one lemon half, then squeeze the
other half into the cavity. Season to taste inside and out with salt and
pepper. Rub the chicken with the fat.

Spoon the stuffing into the cavity. Tie the drumsticks together with string.
Put the onion into the center of a roasting pan. Put the chicken on top.
Roast for 1 1/4–1 1/2 hours, or until the juices run clear when a skewer is
inserted into a leg, basting occasionally. Add the water halfway through
cooking.

Transfer to a board and allow to rest for 15 minutes, tented with foil. Set
the roasting pan over medium–high heat and bring to a boil, skimming any
foam and fat that rises to the surface. Adjust the seasoning and add more
water if necessary. Remove the stuffing to a separate bowl and transfer the
chicken to a serving platter. Garnish with parsley.

roast goose
with fruity apple stuffing

serves 6–8

30 minutes, plus
40 minutes cooling & resting

2 hours 15 minutes

1 tbsp vegetable oil
1 large onion, finely chopped
4–5 large cooking apples, peeled,
  cored, and sliced
3/4 cup stoned prunes, chopped
1 cup dark or golden raisins
3/4 cup no-soak dried apricots,
  chopped
15 oz/425 g canned cooked peeled
  chestnuts in water, drained
1 tsp chopped fresh thyme or 1/2 tsp
  dried thyme

1–2 tbsp chopped fresh parsley
salt and pepper
1 goose, weighing 8–9 lb/3.6–4 kg
1 tbsp potato flour
1/2 cup apple juice
1 tbsp cider vinegar
1/2 cup water
watercress or fresh parsley,
  to garnish

*Goose-rearing has been a Jewish
occupation in much of Central and
Eastern Europe for centuries.
Known as "Jew's Fowl," not only
was it traditional as the Sabbath
meal, the fat was also rendered for
cooking, the quills and down were
sold, and the liver used for pâté.*

Preheat the oven to 450°F/230°C. Heat the oil in a large skillet over medium–high heat. Add the onion and cook for 5 minutes, or until softened. Add the apples, dried fruit, chestnuts, herbs, and a little water and cook for 2–3 minutes, or until the water evaporates. Season to taste with salt and pepper, remove from the heat, and leave to cool.

Remove excess fat from inside and outside the goose. Cut off the fatty skin flap near the tail. Rub the skin and season the cavity with salt and pepper. Prick the skin all over with a fork. Spoon the stuffing into the cavity. Tie the legs together with string. Place in a roasting pan and roast for 30 minutes.

Reduce the oven to 350°F/180°C. Pour off any fat and prick the skin. Turn the goose on to its breast and roast for 1 hour more, basting occasionally; remove excess fat. Turn the goose on to its back and baste; remove excess fat. Roast for 30 minutes more, or until the juices run clear when a skewer is inserted into a leg. Transfer to a board to rest, tented with foil, for 20 minutes. Remove the stuffing to a serving bowl. Keep warm.

Pour off all but 1 tablespoon of fat. Place the pan over medium heat. Blend in the potato flour. Whisk in the apple juice, vinegar, and water. Bring to a boil, stirring constantly. Reduce the heat and simmer for 5 minutes. Strain into a gravy boat. Transfer the goose to a serving plate and garnish.

turkey schnitzel

serves 4

15 minutes,
plus 30 minutes standing

15–20 minutes

1 lb/450 g turkey breast slices, about
 1/2 inch/1 cm thick
1 1/2 tsp ground cumin
1/2 tsp hot (or mild) paprika
1/2 tsp turmeric
1/2 tsp ground coriander
salt and pepper

2/3 cup all-purpose flour
2 eggs, lightly beaten
1 cup matzo meal or dry
 breadcrumbs
3–4 tbsp vegetable oil, for frying
lemon wedges and fresh parsley
 sprigs, to garnish

Because meat like veal is too expensive or unavailable, Israel produces huge quantities of chicken and turkey and prepares them as they would other meat. Turkey schnitzel is a case in point; this is one of the most frequently prepared dishes in Israel.

Put each turkey slice between 2 sheets of waxed paper or plastic wrap and, using a rolling pin, flatten as thinly as possible.

Combine the cumin, paprika, turmeric, coriander, and salt and pepper to taste in a small bowl. Rub on to both sides of the turkey slices. Leave to stand for 30 minutes.

Put the flour, beaten eggs, and matzo meal into 3 separate shallow bowls. Dip each turkey slice into flour to coat, shaking off any excess. Dip into the egg, coating completely, then into the matzo meal, coating well.

Heat about 3 tablespoons of oil in a large skillet over medium–high heat. Fry the turkey slices in batches for about 2 minutes on each side, or until golden-brown, adding more oil if necessary. Remove to paper towels to drain. Keep warm while cooking the remaining slices. Arrange on plates and garnish with lemon wedges and parsley sprigs.

chicken bombay-style

serves 4

20 minutes

**I hour 45 minutes–
2 hours 15 minutes**

I chicken, weighing 3 lb/1.3 kg, rinsed
   and dried

2–3 tbsp vegetable oil or chicken fat

salt and pepper

I onion, halved and thinly sliced

2 garlic cloves, crushed

2 bay leaves

I cinnamon stick

4–6 whole cloves

4–6 whole cardamom pods

I tbsp garam masala or curry
   powder

I tbsp grated fresh root ginger

1/4 tsp turmeric

I cup chicken stock or water

cilantro leaves, to garnish

basmati rice, to serve

*Bombay has a large Bene Israel
community. This fragrant Sabbath
dish is ideal for long slow cooking
and can be prepared the day
before and reheated.*

Preheat the oven to 250°F/120°C. Remove any excess fat from the
chicken. Using a sharp knife, remove the leg quarters from the chicken and
cut through the joint between the thigh and the drumstick. Remove the
breasts and wings. Remove the smallest wing tips and cut the breasts
crossways in half—one half will include the wings. You will have 8 pieces.
(Reserve the carcass and wing tips for soup or stock.)

Heat the oil in a flameproof casserole over medium–high heat. Season the
chicken to taste with salt and pepper.

Add the chicken pieces and cook for 5–7 minutes, or until golden. Turn and
add the onion and garlic, pushing them in between the chicken pieces.
Sprinkle over the herbs and spices.

Pour in the stock and shake the casserole gently to make sure that the
chicken is not stuck. Cover the casserole tightly and bake in the oven for
1 1/2–2 hours, basting with the sauce occasionally. Add a little more stock if
the liquid is absorbed too quickly.

Arrange the chicken on a serving platter and spoon over the sauce.
Sprinkle with cilantro and serve with basmati rice.

barbecued chicken
israeli-style

serves 6–8

15 minutes,
plus 30 minutes to
prepare the barbecue

35 minutes

4 lb 8 oz–5 lb 8 oz/2–2.5 kg chicken
   pieces
2–3 tbsp olive oil
salt and pepper
2 tbsp ground cumin

I tsp ground cinnamon
I tsp turmeric
I tsp hot or mild chili powder
   or paprika
chopped cilantro or mint

*Barbecued foods are as popular
in Israel as in the US or Australia
and the variety is fantastic. Street
corners sizzle with skewered
meats, chicken, and vegetables,
kabobs, and sausage patties, as
well as the aromatic "Jerusalem
grill" of chicken giblets!*

Put the chicken pieces into a large bowl and drizzle over the oil. Using your
hands, rub the chicken pieces with the oil, coating as evenly as possible.
Sprinkle with salt to taste and toss to coat well.

Combine pepper to taste, cumin, cinnamon, turmeric, and chilli powder in
a small bowl. Sprinkle over the chicken and turn to coat the pieces evenly.
Leave to stand.

Prepare a charcoal barbecue at least 30 minutes ahead. Position a rack
about 5 inches/13 cm above the coals. When all the coals are gray and any
flames have subsided, arrange the legs and thighs on the rack and grill for
10 minutes.

Add the breast pieces to the rack and cook for 8–10 minutes. Turn all the
chicken pieces and cook for 8–10 minutes more. Remove the breast
pieces to a serving platter and keep warm.

Cook the legs and thighs for 5 minutes more, or until the juices run clear
when a skewer is inserted into the thickest part.

Alternatively, cook the chicken joints in the same way in a preheated
griddle pan over medium heat.

Transfer the cooked chicken to a serving platter and sprinkle with
chopped cilantro. Serve hot or cold.

duck with
walnuts and pomegranates

serves 4

10 minutes

25 minutes

4 duck breasts
1 tbsp vegetable oil
salt and pepper
1 large onion, sliced
3–4 tbsp sour pomegranate
   concentrate

1/2 cup water
3/4 cup walnuts, finely chopped
2–3 tbsp sugar, or to taste
fresh parsley sprigs, to garnish
rice, to serve

Pomegranates, one of the most symbolic fruit in Jewish history, have been cultivated throughout the Middle East for centuries. Especially in Iran, pomegranates were used in cooking, eaten raw, and squeezed for juices and syrups.

cook's tip

Pomegranate concentrate is available in specialist Middle Eastern shops. If you cannot find it, use 1 cup pomegranate juice, simmered to reduce by half, and eliminate the sugar.

Using a sharp knife, diagonally slash the layer of fat on the duck breasts.

Heat the oil in a large heavy-bottom skillet over medium–high heat. Add the duck breasts, skin-side down, and cook for 7 minutes, or until the skin is crisp and browned and the fat is released into the skillet. Season to taste with salt and pepper. Turn and cook the other side for 3 minutes, or until lightly colored; the meat will be very undercooked at this stage. Remove to a plate and set aside. Reduce the heat to medium.

Pour off all but 1 tablespoon of the fat and add the onion. Cook for 7 minutes, or until soft and golden, stirring occasionally.

Pour in the pomegranate concentrate and water and add the walnuts, stirring to blend. Add the sugar and stir to dissolve. Return the duck breasts to the skillet and cook for 7 minutes, or until they are medium–rare, or to taste. Taste to check the seasoning. Transfer the duck breasts to individual dinner platters, spoon over the sauce and garnish with parsley. Serve with rice.

glazed roast duck

serves 4

25 minutes

2 hours 5 minutes

1 duck, weighing 5–6 lb/
2.25–2.7 kg, rinsed and dried
salt and pepper
juice of 2 oranges (oranges
reserved)
1 onion, sliced
1 tbsp honey

1 tbsp potato flour
3/4 cup chicken stock or water
1 tbsp cider vinegar
1 tbsp orange marmalade (optional)
watercress, to garnish

*Both the Ashkenazic and Sephardic
communities enjoy duck recipes.
Since duck (and geese) are bred in
Israel for eating and for foie gras
production, it is often found in
Jewish homes, roasted simply or
glazed with orange or grapefruit.*

Preheat the oven to 350°F/180°C. Remove any excess fat from the inside
and outside of the duck. Season the cavity and skin to taste with salt and
pepper. Prick the skin all over with a fork. Put the reserved squeezed
oranges inside the cavity.

Put the slices of onion into a roasting pan and cover with a rack. Arrange
the duck on the rack. Roast for 30 minutes, then baste the duck, pour off
any fat and prick the skin again.

Combine half the orange juice and the honey and pour over the duck.
Continue roasting and basting the duck, skimming off any fat every 15–20
minutes, for 1½ hours, or until the duck is crisp and dark golden-brown
and the juices run clear when a skewer is inserted into a thigh. Transfer the
duck to a serving platter to rest, tented with foil.

Tilt the roasting pan and pour off all but 1 tablespoon of the fat. Set the
pan over medium–high heat and stir in the potato flour. Cook, stirring and
scraping the glaze and juices from the bottom. Stir in the remaining orange
juice, stock, vinegar, and marmalade, if using. Bring to a boil and cook for
3 minutes, or until slightly reduced and syrupy. Taste the gravy to check
the seasoning.

Pour, or if you like a smooth gravy, strain the gravy into a gravy boat.
Quarter the duck and arrange on a serving platter with the watercress.

stuffed squab
chickens moroccan-style

 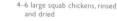

serves 4–6

20 minutes, plus
15 minutes standing & resting

1 hour 15 minutes

4–6 large squab chickens, rinsed
  and dried
2 tbsp olive oil
1/2 tsp hot paprika
1/2 tsp ground ginger
4 tbsp water

couscous stuffing

2 tbsp olive oil
1 onion, finely chopped
2 garlic cloves, finely chopped
1 tbsp grated fresh root ginger
1 1/2 cups quick-cooking couscous
1 tsp ground cumin

1/2 tsp ground cinnamon
1/2 tsp turmeric
1/2 tsp cayenne pepper
1/2 cup raisins or golden raisins
2 oz/55 g no-soak dried apricots,
  diced
1 cup tomato juice or crushed
  tomatoes
8 fl oz/225 ml boiling water
salt and pepper
4 tbsp chopped fresh mint or parsley
fresh mint or parsley sprigs, to
  garnish

*Jews in Morocco make a tasty
stuffing of couscous and North
African spices for poultry. Use to
stuff squab chicken, chicken, or
even lamb. If you prefer, bake in an
oiled dish alongside the meat (bake
any leftover stuffing in this way).*

Preheat the oven to 375°F/190°C. To prepare the stuffing, first heat the oil
in a large skillet over medium–high heat. Add the onion and cook for 2–3
minutes. Add the garlic and ginger and cook for 2–3 minutes more, or until
the onion is softened.

Stir in the couscous, then the spices, dried fruit, tomato juice, water, and
salt and pepper to taste. Remove from the heat, stir in the mint and leave
to stand, covered, for 5 minutes. Leave to cool to room temperature.

Rub each squab chicken with oil, paprika, ginger, and salt and pepper to taste.
Spoon the stuffing loosely into each cavity. Tie the legs together with string.

Roast the squab chickens in a lightly oiled roasting pan for 1 hour, or until
crisp and golden and the juices run clear when a skewer is inserted into a
thigh. Remove to a board to rest, tented with foil, for 10 minutes.

Set the roasting pan over medium heat, add the water, and bring to a boil,
scraping up all the bits on the bottom. Transfer the squab chickens to a
serving platter and spoon over the pan juices. Garnish with mint sprigs.

fricassee of
chicken wings

serves 4

20 minutes

1 hour 10 minutes

2 lb 4 oz/1 kg meaty chicken wings
1 1/3 cups all-purpose flour, plus extra
   if necessary
1/2 tsp salt
pepper
1/2 tsp hot or mild paprika
1 lb/450 g chicken gizzards
   (see Cook's Tip)

2–3 tbsp vegetable oil or schmaltz
4 cups chicken stock or water
1 lb/450 g carrots, sliced
2 tbsp chopped fresh parsley
rice or dumplings, to serve (optional)

When German Jews began to cook the popular French chicken fricassee, they used rendered chicken fat—schmaltz—instead of butter and water or chicken broth instead of cream in order to conform to Jewish dietary laws.

cook's tip

If you prefer not to use gizzards, omit them and increase the chicken wings by the same amount.

Remove the tips of the chicken wings and trim any excess fat (reserve the wing tips for soup or stock). Put the flour, salt, pepper to taste, and paprika into a heavy-duty plastic freezer bag and twist to seal. Shake to blend.

Working in batches, add the chicken wings to the flour mixture in the bag, twist to seal and shake gently to coat. Remove to a plate and continue coating the chicken wings. Working in the same way, coat the chicken gizzards and add to the plate.

Heat the oil in a large skillet over medium–high heat. Working in batches, add the chicken wings and cook for 4–5 minutes, or until well browned, turning once. Transfer to a large pan and continue with the remaining chicken wings and gizzards.

Add any remaining seasoned flour to the fat in the skillet and stir until blended and lightly colored. Gradually whisk in the stock and bring to a boil, stirring to loosen any crispy bits from the bottom. Skim any foam that rises to the surface. Pour, or if you prefer strain over the chicken wings and gizzards and transfer to the heat.

Simmer over medium–low heat, covered, for 35 minutes, stirring once or twice. Add the carrots, pushing them into the gravy, and continue cooking for 15 minutes, or until the chicken wings, gizzards, and carrots are tender. Stir in the parsley and serve immediately with rice or dumplings, if you like.

tongue with
sweet-and-sour raisin sauce

serves 6–8

15 minutes,
plus 8 hours 15 minutes
soaking & cooling

3 hours 50 minutes

1 pickled beef tongue, weighing
    4 lb/1.8 kg, soaked overnight in
    several changes of cold water
6–8 whole cloves
1 tbsp black peppercorns
1 bay leaf
1 cinnamon stick

sweet-and-sour sauce
1 tbsp chicken fat or vegetable oil
2 onions, thinly sliced

1 tbsp all-purpose flour or
    potato flour
3–4 whole cloves
½ cinnamon stick
½ cup tomato sauce or crushed
    tomatoes
2–3 tbsp red or white wine vinegar
1 tbsp mustard, preferably German
2–3 tbsp soft light brown sugar
½ cup raisins

The Old Testament tells the story of Abraham preparing a great delicacy for the angels—tongue with mustard. Tongue remains a special symbol for Jews. This dish is traditional at Sukkoth, the harvest festival, celebrated in October.

cook's tip

For fresh tongue, there is no need to soak. Additional salt can be added. Leftover tongue makes delicious sandwiches on rye bread with mustard.

Put the tongue into a large pan and cover with cold water. Bring to a boil over high heat and boil for 5 minutes, skimming any foam that rises to the surface. Drain and rinse, then return the tongue to the pan. Cover with cold water and add the cloves, peppercorns, bay leaf, and cinnamon stick. Bring to a boil again. Reduce the heat to low and simmer for 3½ hours, or until tender when pierced with a knife. (Top up with water, if necessary, to keep the tongue covered.) Remove from the heat.

Leave the tongue until cool enough to handle. Remove the tongue from the liquid and, using a sharp knife, peel off the tough skin and gristle at the back of the tongue. Reserve 2½ cups of the cooking liquid.

Prepare the sauce. Heat the fat in a large pan over medium heat. Add the onions and cook for 7 minutes, or until soft and beginning to color. Sprinkle over the flour and cook for 1 minute, or until smooth, stirring.

Gradually whisk in the reserved cooking liquid (do not add additional salt) until a smooth thickened sauce forms. Add the remaining sauce ingredients and simmer for 10 minutes. Remove the cloves and cinnamon stick, and taste for seasoning. Serve the tongue in slices with sauce spooned over.

mexican **tzimmes**

serves 8

25 minutes

2 hours 30 minutes

4–6 tbsp chicken fat or vegetable oil

3 lb 8 oz/1.6 kg boneless brisket, rinsed and dried

1–2 tbsp all-purpose flour

2 onions, thinly sliced

2 garlic cloves, crushed

1 lb 12 oz/800 g canned peeled plum tomatoes, chopped (juice reserved)

1 large ripe mango, pitted, peeled, and flesh mashed

1 fresh red chile, seeded and chopped

1 tsp ground cumin

1 cinnamon stick

2 bay leaves

2 tbsp honey

1 tsp salt

4 carrots, sliced

2 sweet potatoes or yams, peeled and cut into chunks

1 1/2 cups stoned no-soak prunes

8 oz/225 g canned red kidney beans, rinsed and drained

2–4 tbsp chopped cilantro, plus leaves to garnish

A tzimmes is a slow-cooked dish of meat or vegetables, sweetened with carrots and fruit, the most famous being Carrot Tzimmes (see page 147). Jews who migrated to Mexico and South America used local ingredients such as mango and sweet potato as sweeteners.

Heat 2–4 tablespoons of the fat in a large flameproof casserole over medium–high heat. Dust the beef with flour. Add to the casserole. Cook for 10–12 minutes, or until well browned on all sides. Remove to a plate.

Add the remaining fat, if necessary, and onions and cook for 4 minutes, or until beginning to soften. Stir in the garlic, then the tomatoes and their juice, stirring to scrape up any meat juices. Add the mango, chile, cumin, cinnamon stick, bay leaves, honey, and salt. Bring to a boil, stirring.

Return the beef to the casserole. Add enough water to cover. Reduce the heat to low and simmer, covered, for 1 1/2 hours. Add more water if needed.

Add the vegetables, prunes, and beans and continue to cook, covered, for 30 minutes more, or until the meat is tender when pierced with a fork. Remove the beef to a serving dish and tent with foil.

Briskly simmer the gravy for 5–6 minutes, or until reduced and slightly thickened, and stir in the coriander. Serve the beef in thin slices with the vegetables, prunes, and gravy spooned over. Garnish with cilantro leaves.

sweet-and-sour
stuffed cabbage

serves 6–8

30 minutes, plus
52 hours freezing & thawing

1 hour 45–55 minutes

1 savoy cabbage (see Cook's Tip)
1 tbsp vegetable oil
1 onion, finely chopped
2 garlic cloves, finely chopped
2 lb 4 oz/1 kg ground beef
  (not lean)
1 tsp salt
pepper
3½ tbsp tomato ketchup
2 eggs, beaten
2–3 tbsp chopped fresh dill
½ cup long-grain rice

sweet-and-sour sauce

1 lb 12 oz/800 g canned peeled plum
  tomatoes, chopped (juice reserved)
14 oz/400 g canned crushed
  tomatoes
½ cup tomato ketchup
salt and pepper
2 onions, thinly sliced
grated zest and juice of 1 lemon
4–5 tbsp soft light brown sugar
1 cup raisins or golden raisins
fresh dill sprigs, to garnish

*There are many versions of stuffed
cabbage in Eastern European
Jewish cooking. This Russian-Polish
version is usually served with rice,
but it is also good with mashed
potatoes. This is a traditional
Sukkoth (harvest festival) dish in
many Ashkenazic homes.*

cook's tip

*Freeze the cabbage two days
ahead and thaw overnight, to
soften the leaves and make them
easier to separate.*

Preheat the oven to 325°F/160°C. Core the cabbage and separate the
leaves. Remove and discard any heavy cores from the leaves.

Heat the oil in a large skillet over medium–high heat. Add the onion and
cook for 3–5 minutes, or until beginning to soften. Stir in the garlic and
remove from the heat to cool.

In a large bowl, mix together the beef, salt, pepper to taste, ketchup, eggs,
dill, rice, and the onion mixture. Arrange a cabbage leaf on the work
surface. Place 1–2 tablespoons of the meat mixture (depending on the leaf
size) in the center. Fold one end of the leaf over the filling, then fold the
sides over. Roll up the leaf to enclose the filling. Arrange on a baking sheet,
seam-side down, and continue with the remaining filling and leaves.

Combine the sauce ingredients in a roasting pan and bring to a boil over
medium–high heat. Simmer for 10–15 minutes, stirring frequently. Remove
from the heat, add the rolls, seam-side down, and spoon over the sauce.
Add a little water if necessary to just cover. Cook, tightly covered, for
1½ hours, basting occasionally. Transfer to a serving platter. Garnish with dill.

stuffed lamb shoulder

serves 6

25 minutes

1 hour 30 minutes

1 shoulder of lamb, weighing
    about 5 lb 8 oz/2.5 kg, boned
    and trimmed
2 tbsp olive oil
2 tbsp honey
1 tbsp potato flour, blended with
    4 tbsp water
1 cup beef or chicken stock
1 tbsp cider or red wine vinegar

stuffing

1 tbsp olive oil
1 onion, finely chopped
2 garlic cloves, finely chopped

1 cup lean ground lamb
1/2 cup long-grain rice
1/2 cup water
salt and pepper
1 tsp ground cumin
1 tbsp chopped cilantro
1/2 cup chopped almonds
3/4 cup raisins
12 no-soak dried apricots, chopped
1 egg, lightly beaten
watercress, to garnish (optional)

*Lamb is a popular choice for
Sephardic Passover Seder because
lamb was so plentiful in the
Sephardic lamb-producing
communities and was at its best in
springtime. As the hindquarters of
lamb and beef are not kosher, the
shoulder is the preferred cut.*

Preheat the oven to 350°F/180°C. Prepare the stuffing. Heat the oil in a
large skillet over medium–high heat. Add the onion and cook for 3–5
minutes, or until beginning to soften. Add the garlic and ground lamb and
cook for 4–5 minutes, stirring to break up the meat. Stir in the rice and
cook for 4–5 minutes, or until translucent, stirring frequently.

Stir in the water, salt and pepper, and cumin. Cook, covered, over medium–
low heat for 12–15 minutes, or until the liquid is absorbed and the rice is
just tender. Remove from the heat. Add the remaining stuffing ingredients.

Open the meat out flat, skin-side down. Spread over the stuffing. Roll up
tightly and secure with string. Brush with oil. Place on a rack in a roasting
pan. Roast for 50 minutes for medium. Brush with honey 15 minutes
before the end. Transfer to a serving plate to rest, tented with foil, for
15 minutes.

Pour off all but 2 tablespoons of the fat. Set the pan over medium–high
heat. Whisk in the potato flour mixture, stock, and vinegar. Bring to a boil,
stirring, then simmer for 8 minutes, or until thickened. Serve with the lamb.

pot-roasted brisket

with onion gravy

serves 8–10

20 minutes

3 hours 45 minutes

3–4 tbsp vegetable oil
5–6 lb/2.25–2.7 kg flat-cut, boneless
   brisket, trimmed, rinsed, and dried
6 onions, thickly sliced
6 garlic cloves, finely chopped
1 cup tomato juice or crushed
   tomatoes

salt and pepper
½ tsp dried thyme
½ tsp paprika
1 bay leaf
6 carrots, cut into thick slices
fresh parsley sprigs, to garnish

This Russian-Jewish favorite makes a good alternative to chicken for a Friday night. Because Jewish men were meant to fulfil their marital obligations, at least on Friday night, rabbis suggested using more garlic as it was considered to be an aphrodisiac.

Preheat the oven to 325°F/160°C. Heat 2 tablespoons of the oil in a large heavy-bottom flameproof casserole over medium–high heat. Add the beef and cook for 10–12 minutes, or until well browned on all sides. Remove to a plate.

Add the remaining oil and onions. Cook for 5–7 minutes, or until the onions are softened and beginning to color, stirring occasionally. Add the garlic and cook for 30 seconds. Add the tomato juice, stirring to scrape up any meat juices. Add salt and pepper to taste, thyme, paprika, and bay leaf.

Return the beef to the casserole, pushing it into the onion mixture. Add enough water to cover the beef. Bring to a boil, skimming any foam that rises to the surface.

Cook in the center of the oven, tightly covered, for 3¼ hours, or until the beef is tender when pierced with a fork. Baste occasionally with the pan juices, adding a little more water if necessary. Add the carrots, pushing them into the liquid, 30 minutes before the end of the cooking time.

cook's tip

This dish is always best prepared a day ahead, the gravy degreased and reheated.

Remove to a heatproof surface and carefully transfer the meat to a cutting board. Tent with foil. Bring the gravy to a boil over medium–high heat and cook until reduced and slightly thickened. Carve the meat into slices, spoon the carrots around the meat, and spoon over a little gravy. Garnish with parsley sprigs and serve the remaining gravy separately.

cholent

serves 8–10

20 minutes,
plus 8 hours soaking

11–13 hours 15 minutes

2 tbsp vegetable oil

3 lb/1.3 kg boneless brisket, or flanken (see page 14), or some of both, cut into large cubes

4 onions, halved and sliced

4–6 garlic cloves, chopped

2 cups dried white beans, such as cannellini, soaked for at least 8 hours

1½ cup pearl barley

10 large potatoes, peeled and quartered

1–2 tsp dried thyme

1 tsp paprika

2 tsp salt

pepper

2 bay leaves

2 tbsp sugar

6 tbsp water

1 lb/450g kosher salami, cubed (optional)

Cholent is the traditional long-cooked stew made to simmer overnight from Friday to Saturday at noon after the service in the synagogue. Dating back to biblical times, the ingredients and flavors vary, but all Jewish communities have a favorite recipe.

Heat the oil in a large flameproof casserole over medium–high heat. Add the beef and cook for 8 minutes, until browned on all sides—you may need to work in batches. Remove to a plate.

Add the onions to the casserole and cook for 10 minutes, or until softened and lightly colored, stirring frequently. Stir in the garlic and cook for 30 seconds. Spread the onions evenly over the bottom of the casserole.

Drain and rinse the beans. Layer over the onions. Layer in the beef, barley, and potatoes and add the thyme, paprika, salt and pepper to taste between each layer. Tuck in the bay leaves. Remove from the heat.

Put the sugar into a small heavy-based pan. Add 2 tablespoons of the water, stirring gently. Cook over high heat, without stirring, for 2 minutes, or until the sugar turns a dark caramel color. Remove from the heat. Holding the pan away from you, pour in the remaining water. Return to the heat, swirling to dissolve the caramel, then pour into the casserole.

Add enough water to cover all the ingredients and return to high heat. Bring to a boil, skimming any foam that rises to the surface. Reduce the heat and simmer for 30 minutes, skimming frequently, adding more water if necessary. Meanwhile, preheat the oven to 225°F/110°C. Add the salami, if using. Transfer to the oven and cook, very tightly covered, for 10–12 hours or overnight. Serve straight from the casserole.

...

shashlik

serves 6

30 minutes,
plus 6 hours chilling

15 minutes

4 lb 8 oz/2 kg boneless lamb
 shoulder, fat trimmed and cut into
 2-inch/5-cm cubes
4–6 small onions, cut into eighths
 with the root end left intact
1 lb/450 g cherry tomatoes
1 large red or yellow bell pepper,
 seeded and cut into
 1-inch/2.5-cm pieces

marinade

3/4 cup extra virgin olive oil
grated zest and juice of 1 large or
 2 small lemons

2 tbsp chopped fresh rosemary
 or mint
4–6 scallions, finely chopped
4–6 garlic cloves, finely chopped
1 tsp salt
pepper
1 small fresh red chile, seeded and
 finely chopped (optional)
fresh rosemary or mint sprigs,
 to garnish
Yogurt-Cucumber Salad (see Cook's
 Tip) or Israeli Salad (see page 46),
 to serve

*The ancient method of cooking
skewered meat over an open wood
or charcoal fire was popular in
Russia, the Balkans, and the Middle
East. Today, skewers of all kinds are
found sizzling on street vendors'
barbecues from Israel to New York.*

cook's tip

*Serve with Yogurt-Cucumber Salad:
combine 1 cup Greek yogurt with
1 long cucumber, peeled, seeded,
and chopped, 2 crushed garlic
cloves, and a handful of chopped
fresh mint. Season to taste with
salt and pepper.*

Combine the marinade ingredients in a large non-metallic bowl and stir until blended. Add the cubes of lamb and toss gently to coat. Refrigerate, covered, for at least 6 hours or overnight, stirring occasionally.

Prepare a charcoal barbecue at least 30 minutes ahead. Position a rack about 5 inches/13 cm above the coals. Thread the lamb cubes on to flat metal skewers (flat skewers prevent the meat from twisting), leaving a little space between the pieces so that the meat cooks evenly. Thread the onions, tomatoes, and bell pepper on to separate skewers.

When all the coals are gray, arrange the lamb skewers on the rack over the center of the coals and cook for 15 minutes, turning and basting occasionally with the remaining marinade. Halfway through their cooking time, add the vegetable skewers and cook, basting occasionally, until tender.

Arrange the skewers on a long serving platter or on individual plates and garnish with the herb sprigs. Serve with Yogurt-Cucumber Salad or Israeli Salad.

meatloaf

serves 6

20 minutes,
plus 30–35 minutes
cooling & resting

1 hour 15 minutes–
1 hour 30 minutes

1 tbsp vegetable oil
1 onion, finely chopped
2 garlic cloves, finely chopped
1 lb 8 oz/675 g fresh ground beef
(not lean)
1 carrot, grated
generous 1 cup fresh white bread
crumbs
2 eggs, lightly beaten
1½ tsp salt
pepper

1 tbsp Worcestershire or
soy sauce
2/3 cup tomato ketchup, plus
2 tbsp for glazing
½ tsp dried thyme or oregano
2–3 tbsp chopped fresh parsley

garnish

sliced tomatoes

parsley sprigs

Meatloaf, or klops, is an old Jewish standby, often served at Friday night suppers as a change from chicken. Although common the world over, it is particularly favored by Russian-Jewish New Yorkers. Do not use lean ground beef; the fat is necessary for a moist loaf.

variation

A tasty variation is to substitute crushed tomatoes for the ketchup and medium oatmeal for the bread crumbs.

Heat the oil in a medium frying pan over medium heat. Add the onion and cook for 7 minutes, or until softened and golden, stirring frequently. Add the garlic and cook for 1 minute. Remove from the heat to cool.

Preheat the oven to 350°F/180°C. Lightly grease a 9 × 5 × 3-inch/23 × 13 × 7.5-cm loaf pan. Put the ground beef into a large mixing bowl and add the onion mixture, grated carrot, and bread crumbs. Toss lightly to combine. Add the eggs, salt, pepper to taste, Worcestershire sauce, ketchup, and herbs. Using a fork or your hands, mix the ingredients together until well blended; do not overwork or the mixture will be too compact and dry.

Spoon the mixture evenly into the loaf pan, smoothing the surface. Bake for 1–1¼ hours, or until the edges begin to shrink from the sides. Baste the top occasionally with the fatty juices. About 10 minutes before the end of the cooking time, brush or smooth over the 2 tablespoons of ketchup to glaze.

Remove to a heatproof surface and leave to rest, tented loosely in foil, for 10–15 minutes. Pour off any excess fat that has not been absorbed. Serve slices from the pan or turn out on to a serving plate, garnish and cut into thick slices and serve.

oven-baked salmon
with avocado dill mayonnaise

serves 10–12

30 minutes,
plus 30–45 minutes standing

30 minutes

2–3 tbsp vegetable oil
1 whole fresh salmon, weighing 5–6 lb/
2.25–2.7 kg, cleaned and scaled,
with head and tail left intact, rinsed
and dried
salt and pepper
1 lemon, quartered
2–3 scallions
1 bunch each fresh parsley and dill

mayonnaise

1 large avocado, pitted, peeled and cut
into pieces
1 cup good-quality or home-made
mayonnaise
2–3 tbsp chopped fresh dill
juice of 1 lemon
1/4 teaspoon cayenne pepper

Fish has always been a mainstay of the Jewish diet. So much fish from the Sea of Galilee was sold in the Jerusalem market that the nearby gate was called "Fish Gate." Since the advent of salmon farming, salmon has replaced carp as the most common "Jewish" fish.

Preheat the oven to 400°F/200°C. Brush half the oil on to a large piece of extra-wide foil. Place the fish in the center. Season the cavity well with salt and pepper. Squeeze the lemon quarters over and inside the fish, then tuck into the cavity with the scallions and herbs. Brush the top of the fish with the remaining oil. Fold together the long edges of the foil over the fish, then the short edges, to form a large loose envelope.

Slide on to a large baking sheet and bake for 30 minutes. Turn off the oven and leave the fish for 15 minutes. Remove the fish from the oven and leave to cool for 15 minutes more, then unwrap. If cooked, the flesh will be just opaque and flake apart with a fork. If not done, rewrap and return to the warm oven for 15 minutes more.

Transfer to a board and fold back the foil. Drain any juices. Using a sharp knife, carefully peel off and discard the skin, pulling out the fins as you go. If you like, gently scrape off the "brown" meat down the center. Gently flip the fish over and repeat on the other side. Carefully slide on to a platter. Cover with a piece of plastic wrap pressed against the flesh.

cook's tip

Remove the skin from the salmon while the fish is still warm, otherwise the skin will stick.

Prepare the mayonnaise. Put the avocado and mayonnaise into a food processor and process until very smooth. Add the dill, lemon juice, and a pinch of cayenne pepper. Season to taste with salt and pepper. Scrape into a serving bowl and dust with cayenne pepper. Serve with the salmon.

cold fried fish

serves 6

25 minutes,
plus 1 hour 15 minutes
standing & cooling

25 minutes

3 lb/1.3 kg fish fillets or steaks, such
    as haddock, cod, plaice or halibut,
    or a combination, rinsed and dried

salt and pepper

1 1/3 cups all-purpose flour

2–3 eggs, beaten

1 cup matzo meal

vegetable oil, for deep-frying

fresh parsley sprigs, to garnish

lemon wedges, to serve

*In the 1860s, a combination of
Ashkenazic and Sephardic Jews in
the fish trade in London's East End
mingled with the Irish immigrants
who ran the potato shops and fish
and chips was born. While fish and
chips became the British national
dish, Jews favored cold fried fish.*

cook's tip

*A mixture of half-medium and half-
fine matzo meal makes the right
combination for maximum crunch.*

Arrange the fish on a large platter, sprinkle with salt and leave for 30–45 minutes, covered, or in the refrigerator. Drain off the water that has drained out and dry well.

Put the flour into a shallow soup plate or dish and season to taste with salt and pepper. Put the eggs into a separate dish and season to taste with salt and pepper, then put the matzo meal into a third dish and season to taste with salt and pepper. Dip each piece of fish first into the flour, tapping to shake off any excess, then into the beaten egg , covering completely, and finally into the matzo meal, turning to coat well and evenly.

Heat about 3 inches/7.5 cm of oil in a deep-fat fryer, wok, or large wide pan to 350–375°F/180–190°C, or until a cube of bread browns in 30 seconds. Working in batches, fry the fish pieces (3–4 at a time) for 5–7 minutes, depending on the thickness of the pieces, turning to brown on all sides. Transfer to paper towels to drain. Add more oil if necessary.

Arrange the fish on a large serving platter and store in a cool place, loosely covered with foil. (Do not refrigerate if possible, as this will cause the fish coating to lose its crispness.) Serve with lemon wedges, garnished with parsley sprigs.

cold sweet-and-sour salmon

serves 4

15 minutes

40 minutes

4 salmon steaks or fillet pieces, about
    6–8 oz/175–225 g each and 1
    inch/2.5 cm thick

salt and pepper

1 onion, thinly sliced

2 carrots, thinly sliced

2 bay leaves

1 cinnamon stick

2 whole cloves

1 tbsp black peppercorns

1³/4 cups water

1/2 cup white wine

2 tbsp vegetable oil

2 tbsp white wine vinegar

1–2 tbsp sugar, or to taste

3 tbsp raisins or golden raisins

1 small fresh red chile, thinly sliced

2 tbsp chopped fresh dill, parsley,
    or cilantro, plus a few sprigs
    to garnish

*Sweet-and-sour fish is very popular
among Eastern European Jews.
Traditionally made with carp, it was
brought to France through Alsace
to become a classic preparation
known as carpe à la Juive—
carp Jewish-style.*

Rinse the salmon under cold running water and dry well with paper towels. Season the salmon to taste with salt and pepper and set aside.

Put the onion, carrots, bay leaves, cinnamon stick, cloves, peppercorns, and water into a large wide sauté pan. Bring to a boil over high heat, skimming any foam that rises to the surface. Reduce the heat to medium and simmer for 15 minutes. Add the wine and oil.

Gently add the salmon pieces and simmer, partially covered, for 10 minutes, or until the fish is a light pink color and opaque; the cooking time will depend on their thickness. Using a skimmer or a fish slice, transfer the fish to a shallow dish.

Bring the cooking liquid to a boil and cook for 5 minutes, or until slightly reduced. Strain into a pan and discard the vegetables, except for a few carrot slices to garnish.

Add the vinegar, sugar, raisins, and chile and simmer for 1–2 minutes. Taste to check the seasoning and stir in the herbs. Remove from the heat and leave to cool slightly. Gently pour over the fish. Serve cold with a little liquid poured over. Garnish with herb sprigs and the reserved carrot slices.

halibut in lemon sauce

serves 4

20 minutes

40 minutes

I onion, sliced
I carrot, sliced
I celery stalk, sliced
I bay leaf
2–3 fresh thyme sprigs
I tsp salt
I tbsp black peppercorns
2–3 tbsp sugar (optional)
1 1/4 cups water

4 halibut steaks or pieces of fillet,
  about 6–8 oz/175–225 g each,
  rinsed and dried
I tsp cornstarch, blended with
  2 tsp water
juice of 2 lemons
3 egg yolks
fresh dill sprigs and lemon slices,
  to garnish

This is a classic among Anglo-Jews—its Sephardic roots are reminiscent of the cold fish in lemon sauce served by Jewish Greeks and Turks. Sephardic Jews who settled in London's East End via Portugal had a lasting influence on Anglo-Jewish fish cookery.

Put the onion, carrot, celery, herbs, salt, peppercorns, sugar, if using, and water into a large sauté pan. Bring to a boil over high heat, skimming any foam that rises to the surface. Reduce the heat to medium and simmer for 15 minutes. Remove and discard the vegetables and herbs.

Add the halibut steaks and simmer for 8 minutes, depending on their thickness, basting frequently; gently pull the flesh away from the bone with a knife to check they are cooked through. Using a skimmer or fish slice, transfer the fish to a shallow dish and tent with foil to keep warm.

Return the liquid to a boil and reduce by about a quarter. Stir the cornstarch mixture into the boiling liquid. Reduce the heat to low.

Whisk the lemon juice into the egg yolks in a small bowl until smooth. Slowly whisk a ladleful of the hot cooking liquid into the egg mixture so that the eggs do not curdle.

Slowly whisk the egg mixture into the sauté pan and cook gently for 2–3 minutes, or until thickened and creamy; do not allow to boil. Strain the sauce into a sauce boat. Arrange the fish on a platter. Spoon over a little sauce. Garnish with dill and lemon. Serve the remaining sauce separately.

barbecued moroccan-style
red snapper

serves 4

15 minutes,
plus 2–3 hours chilling

5 minutes

4 red snapper or halibut fillets
vegetable oil, for oiling

chermoula
4 tbsp extra virgin olive oil
juice of 1 lemon
2–3 garlic cloves, finely chopped
2 tsp ground cumin
2 tsp paprika

½ tsp cayenne pepper, or to taste
salt
2–3 tbsp chopped cilantro
  or mint
fresh mint leaves, to garnish
tomato and red onion salad with
  fresh mint, to serve

North African Jews like to marinate fish before grilling or barbecuing. Chermoula is a classic combination of garlic, olive oil, and cumin, with cayenne for a little heat rather than fresh chiles.

cook's tip

To broil indoors: preheat the broiler. Arrange the fish on a foil-lined baking sheet. Broil about 4 inches/ 10 cm from the heat for 2–3 minutes, or until the skin is crisp and brown. Turn and brush with any remaining marinade. Broil for 1–2 minutes more.

Combine the marinade ingredients in a non-metallic baking dish large enough to hold the fish fillets in a single layer.

Using a sharp knife, diagonally slash the skin side of the fish fillets in 3–4 places. Add the fish fillets to the marinade and turn to coat both sides, rubbing the marinade into the slashes. Refrigerate, covered, for 2–3 hours. Turn the fillets occasionally.

Prepare a charcoal barbecue at least 30 minutes ahead. When all the coals are gray, generously oil the rack and arrange the fish fillets, skin-side down, in the center.

Cook for 2–3 minutes, or until crisp and browned. Using a thin palette knife, carefully loosen the skin from the rack and turn the fillets. Brush with any remaining marinade and cook for 1–2 minutes more, depending on the thickness of the fillets.

Transfer to a serving dish and garnish with mint leaves. Serve with a tomato and red onion salad with mint.

stuffed oven-baked trout
with pomegranates

 serves 4

 30 minutes

25 minutes

4 whole trout, about 10–12 oz/
   280–350 g each, cleaned, scaled,
   rinsed, and dried

vegetable oil, for oiling

2 tbsp butter or margarine, melted

stuffing

3 tbsp extra virgin olive oil

1 onion, finely chopped

2 garlic cloves, finely chopped

1/2 cup shelled and skinned pistachios

4 tbsp chopped fresh parsley
   or cilantro

1/4–1/2 tsp ground cardamom

2–3 tbsp sour pomegranate
   concentrate or 4 tbsp
   pomegranate juice or lemon juice

salt and pepper

1 ripe pomegranate

Since trout farms have been established in the Galilee area of Israel, this traditional Western fish has become very popular. Young Israeli chefs are experimenting with indigenous and new ingredients in a kind of Jewish fusion cooking.

Preheat the oven to 400°F/200°C. Prepare the stuffing. Heat 1 tablespoon of the oil in a medium skillet over medium–high heat. Add the onion and cook for 3–5 minutes, or until beginning to soften. Stir in the garlic and cook for 1 minute.

Stir in the pistachios, parsley, cardamom, pomegranate concentrate, and the remaining oil. Season to taste with salt and pepper.

With a sharp knife, slice off the top of the pomegranate. Score the thick skin into about 6 wedges and pull apart into sections. Carefully scoop the seeds into a small bowl, removing any white pith and reserving any juice. Add about three-quarters of the seeds to the stuffing and stir to combine.

Oil a shallow baking dish large enough to hold the fish. Season to taste with salt and pepper inside and out. Diagonally score 2–3 times on each side. Spoon one-quarter of the stuffing into each fish. Arrange in the dish.

Drizzle with the melted butter. Bake for 15 minutes, or until the flesh is opaque and just flakes when pierced with the tip of a knife. Transfer to a serving plate. Sprinkle with the remaining pomegranate seeds and juice.

light dishes & accompaniments

One of the main characteristics of Jewish food is the separation of meat and dairy, so many light meals are based on eggs, vegetables, pastas, and grains because they are pareve, or neutral.

Eggs are symbolic of the cycle of life—a symbol of birth and death. As well as being used to create everyday dishes, eggs are often served at birth celebrations, funerals, and at the Passover Seder. Eggs in Salt Water (see page 134) are served as a reminder of the sacrifices. Smoked Salmon and Scrambled Eggs (see page 114) and Matzo Brie (see page 112) are popular brunch and supper dishes, as are kugels and blintzes, a specialty of the "dairy delis" on New York City's Lower East Side.

Simple vegetables and grains, such as cabbage, potatoes, barley, and cornmeal, are transformed into delicious side dishes or light meals like Sweet-and-Sour Red Cabbage (see page 124) and Latkes (see page 116).

Many traditional accompaniments such as pickled cucumbers, chrein, and zhough are the most evocative of Jewish foods, conjuring up images of cosy family meals or steamy deli lunches and wonderful memories.

vanilla challah
french toast

serves 6

15 minutes,
plus 7 minutes standing

20 minutes

4 eggs
½ tsp salt
1–2 tbsp sugar, or to taste
grated zest and juice of 1 orange
2 tsp vanilla extract
¾–1 cup milk

12 slices Challah (see page 222), about ¾ inch/2 cm thick
butter or margarine, for frying
confectioners' sugar, for dusting
jelly, syrup, or honey, to serve

The eggy richness of the Challah loaf makes it ideal for French toast, or "eggy bread." This is a good way to use any leftover Challah from the Sabbath dinner. Soaking the bread makes sure that the inside remains soft and moist while the outside is crisp and golden.

Beat the eggs with the salt, sugar, orange zest and juice, vanilla extract, and ¾ cup of the milk in a large shallow baking dish.

Add the bread slices to the egg mixture in a single layer and leave to stand for 2 minutes. Carefully turn the slices and leave to stand for 5 minutes, or until the liquid is completely absorbed and the bread is soaked through.

Melt 2–3 tablespoons of butter in a large skillet or flat griddle pan over medium heat. Using a fish slice or metal palette knife, transfer the soaked bread slices to the skillet or griddle and cook for 3–4 minutes, or until golden-brown, adding more butter as necessary. You may need to work in batches.

Carefully turn the slices and cook for 2 minutes, or until the underside is crisp and golden-brown, or for 3–4 minutes if you prefer the center of the toast less moist.

Transfer to individual plates or a serving platter and dust with confectioners' sugar. Serve jelly, syrup, or honey separately.

matzo brie

serves 1

10 minutes

6–8 minutes

2 matzos
2 large eggs
salt and pepper
1 tbsp butter

Matzo brie is a popular Passover breakfast or light lunch dish. It can be served scrambled yet very crisp, or allowed to set like a flat omelet and served crisp on the outside and soft inside. Children will like it with jelly, cinnamon, and sugar or syrup.

Break the matzos into a colander (the pieces should not be too small). Run under cold water while preparing the eggs, stirring in the colander frequently to be sure that all the pieces are slightly softened.

In a small bowl, beat the eggs very well with salt and pepper to taste.

Heat the butter in a medium skillet over medium–high heat. When the butter is very hot and sizzling, drain and shake the matzo pieces to remove excess water and add all at once to the skillet.

Immediately pour the beaten eggs over the matzo pieces and begin to spread and stir. Once combined, spread evenly and cook for 2 minutes, or until the underside is crisp. Break up the mixture and stir again, until the crisp pieces are mixed into the softer side. Spoon on to a plate or continue to cook and stir until cooked to taste. Sprinkle with salt and pepper.

Alternatively, do not stir. Add the matzo pieces and egg to the skillet and combine as above, flattening to a "pancake." Cook for 3 minutes, or until the underside is crisp. Using a fork, loosen the edges of the pancake from the side of the skillet and give a sharp shake to release the pancake from the bottom. Slide the pancake on to a plate and flip back into the skillet to cook the other side for 3 minutes. Slide on to a serving plate and sprinkle with salt and pepper to taste.

smoked salmon
and scrambled eggs

serves 4

10 minutes

15 minutes

4 tbsp butter or margarine
1 onion, halved and thinly sliced
10 large eggs
salt and pepper

1 tbsp water (optional)
9 oz/250 g smoked salmon
(lox or "Nova"), diced
fresh parsley sprigs, to garnish

Smoked salmon became the primary luxury food in Jewish communities in Britain and the US in the early 1900s. Now much more affordable, it is one of the most popular deli items for Sunday brunch, especially with scrambled eggs.

variation

Some people prefer the smoked salmon served cold, in slices, on the side. If so, do not dice the salmon but arrange the slices evenly on 4 plates. Scramble the eggs and spoon on to the plates with the salmon. If served in this way, it is nice to garnish with a lemon wedge for squeezing over the salmon. If you like, omit the onions.

Heat half the butter in a large (preferably nonstick) skillet. Add the onion and cook for 8–10 minutes, or until softened and golden.

In a large bowl, beat the eggs with just a little salt (under-salt as the smoked salmon will give a salty flavor), pepper to taste, and water, if you like, to lighten the eggs.

Add the remaining butter to the skillet, then add the egg mixture. Reduce the heat to low and cook the eggs, stirring constantly, until just beginning to set.

Sprinkle over the smoked salmon and continue to cook, stirring, until just set. Spoon on to individual plates and garnish with a few parsley sprigs.

latkes

serves 6–8

15 minutes

15–20 minutes

6 medium potatoes, peeled
1 onion
2 eggs, beaten
³/₄ cup fine matzo meal
    or all-purpose flour

1 tsp salt
pepper
vegetable oil, for frying
apple sauce or sour cream,
    to serve

*Latkes, German potato pancakes,
are always served at Hanukkah,
the festival of lights. Latkes fried in
oil are a symbol of a one-day
supply of oil burning for eight days
when the Temple was cleansed and
rededicated in the days
of the Maccabees.*

Grate the potatoes and onion in a food processor fitted with the grater disk. Turn out on to a clean dish towel and wrap, twisting the edges to squeeze out all the liquid.

Transfer to a large bowl and beat in the eggs and matzo meal. Season to taste with salt and pepper.

Heat about 1 inch/2.5 cm of oil in a large heavy-bottom skillet. Drop tablespoonfuls of the potato mixture into the hot oil and cook for 2 minutes, until well browned on the underside. Turn and cook for 1–2 minutes on the other side, or until well browned.

Transfer to paper towels to drain. Continue with the remaining batter. Serve warm with apple sauce or sour cream. Latkes can be reheated in a moderate oven, if necessary.

cook's tip

*The potatoes will quickly brown
after grating, so use immediately.*

variation

*For Cheese Latkes, add ¹/₂ cup
grated mature hard cheese, such
as Cheddar, to the batter. Take care
when frying as the cheese may
cause the Latkes to stick.*

strawberry-cheese blintzes

serves 6–8

30 minutes,
plus 1 hour chilling

45 minutes

blintzes

scant 1 cup all-purpose flour

1½ cups milk or half milk and half
water, plus extra if necessary

3 large eggs, beaten

½ tsp salt

½ tsp sugar

2 tbsp butter, melted, plus extra
for frying

1 lb/450 g strawberries, sliced

sugar, to taste

grated zest and juice of 1 lemon

filling

2 cups cottage cheese

¾ cup cream cheese, softened

3–4 tbsp sugar, or to taste

1 tsp vanilla extract

*Blintzes, originating from the
Russian blini, are thin crêpe-like
pancakes folded around a cottage
cheese, vegetable, or meat filling,
fried golden and topped with sour
cream, apple sauce, cinnamon, and
sugar, or, as here, with strawberries
or other fruit.*

Prepare the blintzes. Sift the flour into a large bowl and make a well in the
center. Whisk in the milk, eggs, salt, sugar, and melted butter, until a smooth
batter forms. Strain into a measuring pitcher and refrigerate, covered, for
1 hour. Thin with milk or water if necessary.

Meanwhile, prepare the filling. Beat the filling ingredients together with an
electric mixer until smooth and well blended. Set aside.

Heat an 7-inch/18-cm crêpe pan or skillet over medium heat. Brush with
melted butter. Pour enough batter into the pan to just coat the bottom.
Cook for 2 minutes, or until the top looks slightly dry and set and the
bottom is lightly browned. Loosen the edges and carefully turn the
pancake. Cook for 10 seconds. Slide on to a plate and cover with plastic
wrap. Repeat with the remaining batter, stacking the pancakes.

Spoon 1–2 tablespoons of filling down the center of 1 pancake. Fold in the
sides, covering the filling, then fold up the bottom edge and roll up.
Combine the strawberries, sugar, lemon zest, and juice in a bowl.

Heat 2 tablespoons of butter in a large skillet over medium heat. Fry the
blintzes, seam-side down, for 2–3 minutes, or until crisp and golden. Turn
and cook for 2 minutes. Continue with the remaining blintzes. Transfer to
individual plates. Spoon over the strawberries and serve warm.

blinis with
smoked salmon & sour cream

serves 6

25 minutes,
plus 2–3 hours standing

20–25 minutes

4 tbsp water

1½ tsp easy-blend dried yeast

⅝ cup all-purpose flour

1 cup buckwheat flour

½ tsp salt

1 cup milk

2 eggs, separated

2 oz/55 g butter, melted

½ cup sour cream, plus extra to serve

snipped fresh chives, to garnish

4 oz/115 g smoked salmon, thinly sliced, to serve

Little Russian pancakes called blinis make a great base for smoked salmon, and other smoked fish, and sour cream. Sliced cucumber, radishes, scallions, and capers can be stirred into the sour cream.

Pour the water into a small bowl. Sprinkle over the yeast. Leave to stand for 5 minutes, or until it begins to bubble and foam. Meanwhile, sift the flours and salt into a large bowl and make a well in the center. Heat three-quarters of the milk in a pan until lukewarm. Add to the well with the yeast mixture, whisking in the flour from the edges to form a smooth batter. Cover and leave in a warm place for 2–3 hours, or until bubbly.

Beat the remaining milk into the batter. Beat the egg yolks in a separate bowl. Stir into the batter with half the melted butter and sour cream.

In another bowl, beat the egg whites with an electric mixer until stiff peaks form (do not over-beat). Fold into the batter until just blended (it does not matter if a few white lumps remain).

Brush a large skillet or flat griddle pan with some of the remaining butter. Pour small ladles of batter into the skillet or griddle to form small pancakes. Cook for 2 minutes, or until golden and the tops are covered with bubbles. Turn and cook for 1–2 minutes. Continue with the remaining batter. Keep warm in a moderate oven.

Arrange the blinis on a serving platter or individual plates. Top each blini with a little smoked salmon and a little sour cream and sprinkle with chives. Serve with the remaining smoked salmon.

cook's tip

Blinis can be made with all white flour, but will lack the rich nutty flavor that is characteristic.

bombay **potatoes**

serves 6–8

10 minutes

20 minutes

3 lb/1.3 kg waxy new potatoes
1 tbsp salt
vegetable oil, for frying
1/2 tsp ground cumin
1/2 tsp ground medium or hot
   chili powder
1/2 tsp crushed dried chili flakes
1/2 tsp turmeric

1/2 tsp garam masala or curry
   powder
1 tbsp freshly squeezed lemon juice
about 4 tbsp water
1 1/3 cups shelled peas
   (thawed if frozen)
2 tbsp chopped cilantro,
   to garnish

*This dish is typical of the Bene
Israel Jews of Bombay. It makes an
ideal accompaniment to Chicken
Bombay-Style (see page 69).*

Peel or scrub the potatoes and cut into 2.5-cm/1-inch pieces.

Transfer to a large pan and cover with cold water. Add the salt and bring
to a boil over high heat. Reduce the heat and simmer for 7 minutes, or
until just tender, but slightly under-cooked; test by inserting a skewer. Drain
and rinse under cold running water.

Heat about 4 tablespoons of oil in a large skillet. Add the cumin, chili
powder, chili flakes, turmeric, and garam masala and cook, stirring to blend,
for 30 seconds.

Carefully add the potatoes and stir to coat with the spicy oil. Add the
lemon juice and water and cook, covered, for 5 minutes, or until tender,
stirring occasionally.

Stir in the peas and cook for 2–3 minutes, or until the vegetables are
tender and any liquid is absorbed. Spoon into a serving bowl and sprinkle
with the cilantro.

sweet-and-sour
red cabbage

serves 6–8

15 minutes

40–50 minutes

2 tbsp vegetable oil
I onion, halved and thinly sliced
2 dessert apples
I red cabbage, weighing about
   I lb 8 oz/675 g
4 tbsp red wine or fruit-flavored
   vinegar

2–3 tbsp soft light brown sugar
3/4 cup raisins or golden
   raisins (optional)
about 4 tbsp water
salt and pepper

Red cabbage is an important ingredient in German and Hungarian cooking. The Jews in these countries often cooked it with vinegar and sugar to accompany the beef, duck, and goose dishes that were typical.

Heat the oil in a large heavy-bottom pan or wok over medium–high heat. Add the onion and cook for 7 minutes, or until softened and beginning to color.

Meanwhile, peel and core the apples and thinly slice. Add to the onion and cook for 2–3 minutes, or until beginning to soften, stirring occasionally.

Quarter the cabbage and remove the white core at the stem end. Cut lengthwise in half again if necessary to fit the feeder tube of a food processor. Fit the processor with the shredding disk and shred the cabbage. Alternatively, shred the cabbage by hand using a large sharp knife.

Add the cabbage to the onion-apple mixture with the wine, sugar, raisins (if using), and water. Season to taste with salt and pepper and reduce the heat to medium–low.

Simmer, covered, for 20–30 minutes, or until the cabbage is just tender, stirring occasionally. Uncover and increase the heat to medium–high. Cook until the liquid is completely absorbed. Spoon into a serving bowl and serve immediately, or leave to cool and serve at room temperature.

home-made lokshen

serves 4–6

40 minutes, plus
55 minutes standing & drying

7 minutes

2½ cups all-purpose flour, plus extra
    for dusting
½ tsp salt, plus extra for cooking
2–3 eggs, beaten

Probably through their "Italian connection," Jews have been making fresh pasta since before the 16th century. Making its way into Poland via the Italians at the royal courts and central Asia, pasta became known by the Yiddish word lokzyn, or noodles.

Put the flour and salt into a food processor and, with the machine running, add about two-thirds of the beaten eggs, until a dough forms. If the dough is too firm and dry, add more egg, a little at a time, and process again until a soft dough forms (the dough should be just flexible, not sticky). Turn out on to a floured work surface and knead for 12 minutes, or until smooth and elastic. Leave to relax, covered with an inverted bowl, for 30 minutes.

Cut the dough in half and, working with one half at a time, roll out on the lightly floured work surface as thinly as possible into a 14-inch/35-cm square. Transfer to a large floured baking sheet and repeat with the second piece of dough. Leave to dry for 25 minutes.

When the dough surface looks dry, fold the dough loosely in half, then in half again and repeat until you have a loosely folded strip of dough about 2 inches/5 cm wide. With a sharp knife, slice crosswise, straight down in one movement without dragging the knife, into strips ⅛–½ inch/3 mm–1 cm wide, depending on the recipe.

Unroll the noodles, gently shaking to separate. Leave to rest for 1 minute. If not using immediately, hang the noodles over a wooden rack to dry.

Bring a large pan of salted water to a boil. Add the noodles all at once, cover and return to a boil. Cook for 2 minutes for wide noodles, slightly less for thin ones. As soon as the noodles rise to the surface they are cooked. Drain into a colander and serve in soup, toss with butter and cheese, or refresh under cold water to use in other recipes.

cabbage & noodles

serves 4–6

10 minutes

35–40 minutes

2–3 tbsp chicken fat, vegetable oil,
    butter or margarine, plus extra
    to serve (optional)
1 onion, chopped
1 small or ½ large green cabbage

salt and pepper
6 oz/175 g wide egg noodles

*This Ashkenazic recipe was popular
with German and Hungarian Jews
who made great use of green
cabbage and onions—vegetables
that survived and could be stored
throughout the long cold winters.*

variation

*For a Hungarian-style version, do
not brown the onions. Cook for
5 minutes until softened. Stir
in 1 teaspoon of paprika and
1 teaspoon of caraway seeds, lightly
crushed, and continue as above.*

Heat the fat in a large skillet or wok over medium heat. Add the onion and
cook for 7 minutes, or until softened and beginning to color slightly, stirring
frequently.

Meanwhile, cut the cabbage lengthwise in half and remove the white core.
Turn cut-side down on to a cutting board and shred crosswise into
medium–fine strips.

Add the cabbage and salt and pepper to taste to the skillet and cook over
low heat for 20 minutes, or until the cabbage is tender, stirring frequently.
If the cabbage begins to brown, reduce the heat or add a tablespoon or
two of water.

Bring a large pan of salted water to a boil. Add the noodles and cook for
7 minutes for dried noodles or 2 minutes for fresh (or according to the
packet instructions), or until just tender. Drain well and add to the
cabbage, tossing to mix well. If you like, add a tablespoon of fat to the
vegetables and noodles, taste to check the seasoning, and serve.

chrein

makes about 1 lb 8 oz/675 g

15 minutes

–

1 medium fresh horseradish root
3–4 medium beets, cooked
1 tbsp honey or soft light brown
   sugar
pepper
3/4 cup cider vinegar,
   or to taste

Horseradish is one of the bitter herbs found on the Passover table, recalling the bitterness of the Jews in slavery. Here it is combined with beets in a sauce that Russian Jews call chrein. It accompanies Gefilte Fish (see page 44).

If you like, wear rubber gloves to protect your hands while you prepare the horseradish and beets. Using a swivel-bladed vegetable peeler, peel the horseradish root and trim the ends. Using a food processor fitted with the grating disk, grate the horseradish. Do not remove the cover at this stage—the initial fumes are extremely potent!

Peel the beets and, if necessary, trim them to fit into the feeder tube of the food processor. Grate the beets on to the horseradish.

Carefully scrape the horseradish-beets mixture into a non-metallic bowl. Gently stir in the honey, pepper to taste, and vinegar. If the mixture seems too dry, add a little more vinegar.

Spoon into an airtight jar or container and refrigerate, tightly covered, for up to 1 week. The longer the sauce is stored, the less pungent it will become.

cook's tip

Horseradish varies in strength depending on its origin and length of storage, so taste the mixture after adding the vinegar and season to your taste.

beet eingemacht

makes about 5 cups

15 minutes,
plus 15 minutes cooling

45–50 minutes

3 lb/1.3 kg beets, cooked
2 lemons
1 cup sugar
2/3 cup honey

2 tbsp finely chopped fresh
   root ginger
1/2 cup water
1 cup whole or slivered blanched
   almonds

*This traditional preserve is a
Passover speciality, sometimes
served in a teaspoon on a saucer
of mint tea or on matzo crackers.
Sometimes made with prunes,
walnuts, and lemons, beetroot
eingemacts were most popular in
Eastern Europe.*

cook's tip

*Cut the beet thinly for a jelly-like
consistency, or thicker for a more
solid chutney.*

If you like, wear rubber gloves to protect your hands being stained while
peeling the cooked beets. Thinly slice and set aside.

Using a sharp knife, cut the ends off the lemons, then cut each lengthwise
in half. Thinly slice the lemon halves and remove any pips.

Put the sugar, honey, and ginger into a large stainless steel pan. Add the
water and bring to a boil over medium–high heat. Reduce the heat and
simmer for 7 minutes, or until the sugar is dissolved and the liquid is syrupy,
stirring occasionally.

Carefully add the sliced beets and lemon slices, and stir to combine. Return
to a boil, then reduce the heat and simmer over low heat for 35–40
minutes, or until the mixture is very thick and holds together. Stir and
shake the pan occasionally to prevent sticking. Stir in the almonds and
remove from the heat. Leave to cool slightly.

Prepare preserving jars according to the manufacturer's instructions.
Carefully spoon the mixture into the jars, filling to the top. Leave to cool
completely, then cover with wax disks and lids. Use within 3 weeks.

eggs in salt water

serves 6

10 minutes,
plus 30 minutes soaking

–

3 tsp salt
4 cups water
6 eggs, hard-cooked

This is one of the most important elements on the Passover Seder table. Eggs represent birth and life and salt water symbolizes the tears shed by the Israelites. The combination represents the sacrifice to the temple and is a symbol of mourning for its death.

Shell the hard-cooked eggs.

Stir the salt into the water in a large bowl until dissolved.

About 30 minutes before serving, add the eggs to the water.

To serve, transfer 1 egg and about ½ cup of the water to each of 6 small bowls and pass to each person at the table.

ashkenazic haroset

makes about 1 lb 8 oz/675 g

15 minutes

–

2 dessert apples
¾ cup walnut pieces, finely chopped
¾ cup almonds, finely chopped
¾ cup pitted dried dates, chopped,
plus extra to garnish
2–3 tbsp soft light brown sugar
1 tsp ground cinnamon
¼ tsp ground allspice

3–4 tbsp kosher red wine
grated zest and a little juice from
1 orange or lemon
strips of orange zest, to garnish

*Haroset is a kind of relish always
found on the Passover Seder table.
The chopped fruit and nuts
symbolize the bricks and mortar
used to construct the pyramids of
Egypt and to help sweeten the
bitter herbs on the Seder plate.*

Cut the apples into quarters, core and finely chop.

Combine the nuts, fruit, sugar and spices in a non-metallic bowl.

Moisten with the wine and orange zest and juice. Taste and add more
sugar or wine to taste if necessary.

Spoon into a serving bowl and serve at room temperature or chilled.

variation

*For a Sephardic version: combine
¼ cup each of walnuts, blanched
almonds, and raisins with 1 cup
chopped pitted dates and the
seeds and juice of 1 pomegranate.
Add 1 teaspoon of ground
cinnamon and ½ teaspoon
each of ground ginger, pepper,
cloves, and cardamom. Moisten
with 3–4 tablespoons of orange
juice and 2–3 tablespoons of
sweet kosher red wine.*

zhoug

makes about ¹/₂ cup

5–10 minutes

–

5–6 fresh red or green chiles
3–4 garlic cloves
¹/₂–³/₄ tsp salt
pepper
1 tsp ground cumin
¹/₄ tsp ground cardamom
1–2 tbsp water

Yemenite Jews use this fiery chile paste to season just about everything. Similar to the North African harissa served with couscous, it can also be used as a condiment with kabobs, falafel, and meat sandwiches in pita bread.

If you like, seed the chiles; the seeds carry a great percentage of the heat, but you can leave them in. Try to use rubber gloves when handling chiles and wash your hands and all utensils very well afterward.

Put all the ingredients, except the water, into a food processor and process until a smooth paste forms.

Gradually add the water to soften the consistency.

Store in an airtight jar or container up to 1 week.

uncle john's pickled
cucumbers

makes 5 lb/2.25 kg

20 minutes,
plus 24 hours standing

5 lb/2.25 kg pickling cucumbers
2–3 fresh red chiles, thinly sliced
2–3 fresh green chiles, thinly sliced
2–3 bay leaves
1 tbsp pickling spice
1-inch/2.5-cm piece fresh root ginger,
  peeled and sliced

$^1\!/4$–$^1\!/2$ cup superfine sugar
$^1\!/3$ cup kosher or coarse salt
$^3\!/4$ cup acetic acid
5–5$^1\!/2$ cups boiling water

Pickling developed as a method of food preservation, particularly in the Eastern European Jewish cultures. Jews enjoyed the strong sharp flavors as a contrast to the bland starchy diets available at the time. Pickling was almost essential for survival in Ashkenazic Jewish life.

cook's tip

Acetic acid is a pickling agent and is available from large supermarkets and Jewish delis.

Wash and dry the cucumbers and, if large, cut into quarters or halves. Put them into a very large, non-metallic mixing bowl or casserole.

Sprinkle over the remaining ingredients and pour over the acetic acid. Pour over the boiling water and, using a wooden spoon, gently push the ingredients around (stirring is difficult), until the sugar and salt are dissolved.

Leave to cool to room temperature, then cover with plastic and leave for 24 hours or longer.

Decant into preserving jars with equal amounts of the vegetables and flavorings and ladle over enough pickling liquid to cover. Seal the jars.

the reubens **sandwich**

serves 2

30 minutes

7 minutes

2 tbsp margarine, softened

4 slices "deli" rye bread

4–6 oz/115–175 g cooked salt beef, thinly sliced

⅓ cup bottled sauerkraut, well drained

1 cup grated Gruyère cheese

vegetable oil or margarine, for frying

Pickled Cucumbers (see page 141), to serve

thousand island dressing

1 cup bottled or home-made mayonnaise

2 tbsp ketchup or chili sauce

2 tbsp seeded and finely chopped green bell pepper

2 tbsp finely chopped pimento

2 tbsp finely chopped sweet-and-sour pickled cucumber

Following the great emigration of the 1880s, by the 1920s more than 2 million Jews were working in sweatshops. They bought kosher food from Jewish neighbors, and a great Jewish-American institution, the Jewish deli, was born. It served some fantastic sandwiches.

Prepare the dressing. Mix the dressing ingredients together in a bowl until well blended. Store, refrigerated, in an airtight container for up to 1 week.

Spread the margarine on to one side of each bread slice. Lay margarine-side down. Spread the other sides with 1 tablespoon each of the dressing.

Divide the salt beef between 2 bread slices, tucking in the slices to fit. Divide the sauerkraut and make an even layer over the salt beef, then cover the sauerkraut evenly with the grated cheese. Top with the remaining bread slices, margarine-side out, and press firmly to compress the layers.

Heat a nonstick skillet or ridged griddle pan over medium–high heat. Carefully slide the sandwiches into the pan. Using a fish slice, press down on the tops of the sandwiches. Cook for 3 minutes, or until the undersides are crisp and golden.

Carefully turn, press down again, and cook for 2 minutes, or until golden, the cheese is melted and the beef is hot. Transfer to a cutting board. Cut in half and serve with Pickled Cucumbers.

persian jeweled rice

serves 6

20 minutes, plus 1 hour standing

50 minutes–1 hour

2 1/2 cups basmati rice
1 tbsp salt
2 oranges
1/2 cup sugar
4–6 tbsp vegetable oil

1/4 tsp saffron threads or powder
3/4 cup golden raisins
12 no-soak dried apricots, chopped
1/2 cup shelled and skinned pistachios, chopped

Persian (Iranian) Jews are one of the oldest communities, dating back to Babylonian times. This recipe reflects their great ancient status as wealthy traders in the silk and spice trades. This dish is served at weddings and other special occasions.

Rinse the rice under cold running water, then turn into a bowl and cover with cold water. Stir in the salt. Leave to stand for 1 hour.

Using a swivel-bladed vegetable peeler, remove the zest from the oranges, being careful not to take any white pith with the zest. Shred very finely. Bring a small pan of water to a boil, add the zest and boil for 2 minutes. Drain and rinse, then return the zest to the pan with the sugar and 4 tablespoons of water. Bring to a boil, swirling the pan to dissolve the sugar. Simmer for 10 minutes, or until the zest is translucent and caramelized, then drain.

Bring a large pan of salted water to a boil over high heat. Rinse and drain the rice, then add to the water and boil for 8–10 minutes, or until beginning to soften but still slightly firm. Drain into a strainer.

Add the oil to the pan and return to very low heat. When the oil is warm, stir in the saffron, then stir in the rice. Add the dried fruit, nuts, and drained orange zest, stirring well to coat the rice with the saffron and oil.

Cover the rice with a round of waxed paper and cook for 20 minutes, or until tender. Gently fork into a serving bowl. Alternatively, turn into a greased baking dish and bake in a preheated oven, covered, at 350°F/180°C for 30 minutes.

carrot tzimmes

serves 6

10 minutes

25–30 minutes

2 tbsp butter or vegetable oil
1 lb 8 oz/675 g carrots, sliced
salt and pepper
juice of 1 orange

½-inch/1-cm piece fresh root ginger,
  peeled and cut into thin slivers
2 tbsp honey, or to taste
½ cup water

A tzimmes is a sweetened vegetable or meat dish, but most Jews think of carrots when they hear the word. Served at the New Year (Rosh Hashanah), sliced carrots are symbolic of gold coins, while honey symbolizes the hope of a sweet New Year.

Heat the butter in a wide, deep skillet or pan over medium–high heat. Stir in the carrot slices, then add salt and pepper to taste and the remaining ingredients.

Bring to a boil, then reduce the heat to low and simmer, covered, for 15 minutes, or until just tender. Increase the heat and cook, uncovered, until the liquid is reduced and the carrots well glazed, stirring occasionally.

variation

For spicy Sephardic carrots: omit the orange and ginger. Boil carrots until tender. Drain. Heat the oil. Stir in 1 teaspoon of ground cumin, 1 seeded chopped fresh red chile (or to taste), 1 garlic clove, chopped, and the juice of 1 lemon. Cook, stirring, for 1 minute. Add the carrots and honey and 2–3 tablespoons of water. Cook until the liquid is evaporated and the carrots are tender and well-coated. Sprinkle with 1–2 tablespoons of chopped fresh mint or cilantro.

venetian saffron rice

serves 4

10 minutes,
plus 5 minutes standing

35 minutes

3 tbsp vegetable oil

1 1/2 cups Italian risotto rice, such as Arborio or Carnaroli

4 cups chicken or vegetable stock, preferably home-made

1/2 cup dry white wine

1/2 tsp salt, or to taste

1/2 tsp saffron threads or powder

2 tbsp butter or margarine

1/2 cup freshly grated Parmesan cheese

Rice is a staple of the Sephardic Jewish world, except in North Africa where couscous is king. The Jews of the Venetian Ghetto were dealers in the spice trade and so spices like saffron and turmeric found their way into Jewish cuisine.

cook's tip

To serve with a meat meal, omit the butter and Parmesan and serve as is, or stir in a chopped onion and 4 cups of sliced mushrooms, fried in 1 tablespoon of oil.

Heat the oil in a large, heavy-bottom pan over medium–high heat. Add the rice and stir to coat with the oil. Cook for 3–4 minutes, or until the rice becomes translucent, stirring frequently.

Meanwhile, bring the stock to a boil in a separate pan.

Add the wine to the rice—it will splutter and evaporate almost immediately. Pour in the boiling stock all at once, add the salt, and stir. Bring to a boil, then reduce the heat to very low and simmer, covered, for 25 minutes.

Put the saffron into a small heatproof dish and pour over enough boiling stock to cover. About 5 minutes before the rice is done, drizzle over the saffron and water. Fluff up the rice with a fork to combine.

Stir in the butter and Parmesan cheese and remove from the heat. Leave to stand, covered, for 5 minutes before serving.

knaidlach—matzo balls

makes 36 small balls

15 minutes,
plus 2 hours chilling

25 minutes

3 eggs
6 tbsp chicken fat or vegetable oil
1 tsp salt
2/3 cup cold water

whole nutmeg, for grating, or 1/4 tsp
    ground ginger or cinnamon
1 1/3 cups medium matzo meal
Chicken Soup (see page 21), to serve

*The Yiddish word knaidlach comes
from the German knodel, for
dumpling. Dumplings have been
popular in Eastern European
cooking since the Middle Ages. This
Jewish dumpling made with matzo
meal was devised as a Passover
substitute for bread dumplings.*

In a large bowl, beat the eggs, chicken fat, and salt together until blended.
Whisk in the water.

Grate a little nutmeg into the matzo meal in a separate bowl and stir to
combine. Whisk the matzo meal into the egg mixture to form a soft batter.
Refrigerate, covered, for about 2 hours, or until the mixture is firm.

Using wet hands to prevent sticking, form the mixture into 3/4-inch/2-cm
balls and transfer to a baking sheet. (Matzo balls can be open frozen at this
point, then thawed for 1 hour before cooking.)

Bring the soup to a boil in a large pan over medium–high heat. Gently add
the matzo balls; they will bob to the surface and begin to swell. Simmer
gently for 25 minutes, stirring occasionally. Alternatively, for a clearer soup,
simmer the matzo balls in a large pan of salted boiling water. Transfer to
the soup before serving. Ladle about 3 balls into each bowl of soup.

cook's tip

*You will need to use more soup
than usual to allow for the matzo
balls absorbing some of the liquid.*

variation

*Although delicious, the matzo ball can be considered heavy.
For light, fluffy knaidlach, separate the eggs. Beat the whites
separately until stiff, then beat the yolks until lightened in
color. Slowly beat in the chicken fat or oil, salt, and water. Then
fold in the egg whites until just blended. The mixture can be
chilled as above, but it will deflate slightly, or it can be dropped
by teaspoonfuls into the simmering soup or water.*

spicy tunisian COUSCOUS

serves 4

15 minutes

15–20 minutes

1²/₃ cups quick-cooking couscous
2 tbsp olive oil
1 onion, finely chopped
3–4 garlic cloves, finely chopped
1 fresh red chile, finely sliced,
   or to taste
1 tsp paprika

¹/₂ tsp ground cumin
¹/₂ tsp ground cinnamon
salt and pepper
2 tbsp chopped fresh mint, cilantro
   or parsley, plus a few leaves to
   garnish

Couscous is a fine semolina pasta made from wheat, though it resembles a grain. It is a staple of North Africa, just as pasta is in Italy. Traditionally, couscous was cooked above a simmering stew.

variation

For a more substantial Vegetable Couscous, prepare as above but omit the chile and cinnamon. Add an additional ¹/₂ teaspoon ground cumin, 1 teaspoon ground coriander, 2 seeded chopped tomatoes, 8 oz/225 g chopped zucchini, 14 oz/400 g canned chickpeas, and cayenne pepper to taste, adding a little more water if necessary. Combine with the cooked couscous. Garnish with toasted pine nuts and chopped fresh mint.

Prepare the couscous according to the packet instructions. Set aside.

Meanwhile, heat the oil in a medium skillet over medium–high heat. Add the onion and cook for 5–7 minutes, or until softened and beginning to color, stirring frequently.

Add the garlic, chile, paprika, cumin, cinnamon, and salt and pepper to taste. Cook for 2 minutes. Remove from the heat and stir in the fresh herb.

Stir the onion mixture into the cooked couscous and spoon into a serving dish. Serve hot or at room temperature, sprinkled with a few herb leaves.

romanian mamaliga
with cheese

serves 6–8

10 minutes or 2–3 hours
30 minutes cooling & chilling

25–40 minutes

3 cups fine yellow cornmeal or
  polenta
1 tsp salt
5 cups water

4 tbsp butter or pareve margarine
1 cup cottage cheese, drained and
  strained

Cornmeal, made from maize, was
introduced to Europe from the
newly discovered Americas in the
16th century. Known as polenta in
Italy, cornmeal became so popular
in Romania that it was eaten as a
porridge for breakfast,
lunch, and dinner.

Put the cornmeal and salt into a medium bowl and stir in 1 cup of the cold water until smooth. Bring a large pan filled with 4 cups water to a boil over high heat. Gradually pour the wet cornmeal into the boiling water, stirring to prevent any lumps forming.

Cook, stirring constantly with a wooden spoon, over medium–low heat for 20–25 minutes, or until the cornmeal forms a mushy porridge and the water is absorbed.

Remove from the heat and stir in the butter and the strained cheese. Leave to stand for 1 minute. Stir and spoon into a serving bowl.

Alternatively, cook the cornmeal as above, reducing the water by about 1 cup. Stir in only half the butter and omit the cheese. Pour into a greased 9 x 5 x 3-inch/23 x 13 x 7.5-cm loaf pan and leave to cool. Refrigerate, covered, for 2–3 hours, or until firm and chilled.

Run a sharp knife around the edges of the pan and unmold on to a cutting board. Cut into thin slices.

Heat the remaining butter in a large, heavy-bottom skillet over medium–high heat. Working in batches, add the cornmeal slices and cook for 2 minutes, or until heated through and crisp and golden. Carefully turn and cook for 1 minute more. Serve with roasted poultry and stews.

kasha varnishkes

serves 6–8

 10 minutes

25 minutes

1 ½ cups kasha (buckwheat groats)
1 egg, well beaten
2 ½ cups water (or stock, if serving
   with a meat meal)
½ tsp salt

pepper
2 tbsp butter or vegetable oil
1 large onion, finely chopped
2 cups dried bow-tie pasta

Kasha, buckwheat groats, was a food of the poor Russian and Polish Jews. This hearty, nourishing grain was usually cooked to make a thick porridge. This dish is prepared on Purim, a joyful celebration celebrating the Jews' deliverance from the wicked Persian Haman.

Mix the kasha and eggs together in a bowl then add to a large, heavy-bottom pan and set over medium heat. Cook for 5 minutes, or until the grains are separated and lightly toasted, stirring frequently.

Stir in the water and add the salt and pepper to taste. Reduce the heat to medium–low and cook, covered, for 10 minutes, or until the kasha is tender and has absorbed the liquid.

Meanwhile, heat the butter in a medium skillet over medium–high heat and add the onion. Cook for 7 minutes, or until softened and golden, stirring frequently.

Bring a large pan of salted water to a boil. Add the pasta and cook for 8 minutes, or according to the packet instructions, until tender. Drain and rinse the pasta.

Using a fork, fluff up the kasha, separating the grains. Add the kasha and pasta to the onion, tossing and stirring to combine well. Serve as an accompaniment to pot roast or other meat or poultry dishes.

kreplach

makes about 48 pieces

50 minutes–1 hour,
plus 30 minutes standing

1 hour 15 minutes

1 quantity Home-Made Lokshen
(see page 126)

filling

1 cup cooked beef or
ground beef
1 onion, chopped

½ tsp salt
pepper
1 tbsp chopped fresh dill
1 egg
1 quantity Chicken Soup
(see page 21), to serve

*Kreplach, often called Jewish
won tons, are an important symbol
of Jewish traditional food. Filled
with chopped meat from the shin
of beef used for the soup, they are
served in Chicken Soup on the eve
of Yom Kippur (Day of Atonement)
and on the last day of Sukkoth.*

cook's tip

*The kreplach can be cooked in the
soup, but the soup will be cloudy.*

*Kreplach can be cooked as above
and tossed with butter or oil and
served with a little grated cheese,
or topped with tomato sauce and
fresh herbs.*

Prepare the filling. Put the beef and onion into a food processor and
process until finely chopped; do not over-process or the mixture will be
too pasty. Add the salt, pepper to taste, dill, and the egg and, using the pulse
button, process until blended and a soft mixture holds together.

Roll out the Lokshen dough as directed on page 126, but do not dry. Cut
the dough into 2-inch/5-cm squares. Drop about ½ teaspoon of the filling
on to the center of each square and brush the corners with a little water.
Fold the lower right-hand corner up and over the filling to the upper left-
hand corner, forming a triangle. Press the edges firmly together to seal.

Transfer the kreplach to a lightly floured baking sheet and continue with
the remaining dough and filling. Kreplach can be prepared ahead to this
point and refrigerated overnight.

Bring a large pan of salted water to a boil. Working in batches, add some
of the kreplach and simmer for 12–15 minutes, or until just tender.
Remove to a colander and drain. Continue until all the kreplach are
cooked. Cover and refrigerate or freeze for future use.

To serve, bring the Chicken Soup to a boil in a large pan. Add the kreplach
and simmer for 6–8 minutes to heat through. Serve 2 or more kreplach in
each bowl of soup.

sweet potato, parsnip & carrot
kugel

serves 6–8

15 minutes, plus
15 minutes cooling & resting

55 minutes

4 tbsp butter or pareve margarine

1 onion, finely chopped

2 sweet potatoes

2 large carrots

2 large parsnips

1 cooking apple, peeled, cored, and
quartered

salt and pepper

1 tsp ground cinnamon

1/2 tsp freshly grated nutmeg

1/3 cup soft light brown sugar

4 tbsp honey

4 tbsp water

2 eggs, beaten

1/2 cup matzo meal

2 tbsp vegetable oil

This kugel, made with naturally sweet winter vegetables, is a very popular one. This dish is ideal for Passover, but also makes a good accompaniment to roast duck and turkey. Butternut squash, now widely available, could be substituted for sweet potato.

Preheat the oven to 375°F/190°C. Heat the butter in a large skillet over medium–high heat. Add the onion and cook for 3 minutes, or until beginning to soften, stirring occasionally.

Grate the sweet potatoes, carrots, parsnips, and apple in a food processor fitted with the coarse grating disk. Add to the onion and cook for 5 minutes, or until the vegetables begin to soften, stirring frequently. Remove from the heat and leave to cool slightly.

Season the vegetable mixture with salt and pepper to taste, add the cinnamon, nutmeg, sugar, honey and water, and stir well. Add the beaten eggs and matzo meal and mix well to combine.

Heat the oil in a medium roasting pan or flameproof dish in the oven. When the oil is very hot, turn the mixture into the pan or dish and distribute evenly, smoothing the top (this will give a crisp base as well).

Bake, covered with foil, for 30 minutes. Remove the foil and continue to bake for 15 minutes, or until the vegetables are tender and the top is golden-brown. Remove to a wire rack and leave to rest for 5 minutes before serving.

lemon-scented cheese-noodle
kugel

serves 4–6

15 minutes

1 hour

8 oz/225 g wide egg noodles

4 oz/115 g butter or pareve
  margarine, softened, plus extra for
  greasing

1 cup cream cheese, softened

1 cup cottage cheese

5 eggs, beaten

2 ½ cups pint milk

grated zest and juice of 1 lemon

3–4 scallions, chopped

2–3 tbsp toasted pine nuts (optional)

salt and pepper

freshly grated nutmeg

Kugel, a favorite baked pudding or casserole among Ashkenazic Jews, was traditionally cooked alongside a Cholent (see page 91) as an accompaniment or separate course. Kugels are hugely popular.

cook's tip

For a more modern presentation, bake in individual soufflé dishes and reduce the baking time to about 25 minutes. Serve each person with their own mini kugel.

Preheat the oven to 350°F/180°C. Bring a large pan of salted water to a boil over high heat. Add the noodles, return to a boil and cook for 7 minutes, or according to the packet instructions, until just tender, stirring frequently to avoid sticking. Drain and rinse. Set aside.

Using an electric mixer, cream the butter and cream cheese together in a large bowl until well blended. Gradually beat in the cottage cheese, then the eggs, and milk until well blended.

Stir in the lemon zest and juice, scallions, and pine nuts, if using. Season well with salt, pepper, and nutmeg. Add the cooked noodles and toss gently to mix well.

Turn the mixture into a lightly greased baking dish and distribute evenly, smoothing the top. Bake for 50 minutes, or until set and the top is puffed and golden-brown. Serve hot or at room temperature.

long-cooked ouevos
haminados (hard-cooked eggs)

serves 8

10 minutes

6–8 hours

skins of 8 onions
8 large eggs
1 tsp salt
pepper

2 tbsp olive oil
Hummus (see page 33), tahini, or
  Garlic Mayonnaise (see below),
  to serve (optional)

These long-cooked eggs are one of the most important Sephardic-Jewish foods. Originally cooked in the Hamin, the Sephardic version of the Ashkenazic Cholent (see page 91), they took on a rich nutty color from the onions and beef in the casserole.

Preheat the oven to 225°F/110°C. Put the onion skins into an ovenproof casserole and "nestle" the eggs among the skins.

Sprinkle in the salt and pepper to taste and drizzle over the oil (the oil prevents the water evaporating). Slowly add enough water to cover.

Roast for 6–8 hours, or overnight.

Remove, rinse, and drain the eggs, then leave to cool. Shell and halve the eggs. They should have golden shells and creamy buttery yolks with a golden-colored white. Serve as part of a buffet or as an appetizer with a little Hummus, tahini, or Garlic Mayonnaise (see below), if you like.

Garlic Mayonnaise

Put 4 crushed garlic cloves into a warm bowl and beat in 1 egg yolk with 1 teaspoon of water and the juice of half a lemon. Season with about ½ teaspoon of pepper. Gradually whisk in about 1 cup extra virgin olive oil (or a mixture of olive oil and vegetable oil), drop by drop until the oil is absorbed. Increase the oil to a thin stream, whisking continuously, until a thick creamy mayonnaise forms. Adjust the seasoning and add a little cayenne pepper, if you like.

aunt lucille's caponata

serves 6

10 minutes, plus 4 hours
30 minutes cooling & chilling

40–45 minutes

2 lb 4 oz/1 kg eggplants

extra virgin olive oil, for frying

1 large onion, sliced

3–4 garlic cloves, crushed

3 celery stalks, cut into ½-inch/1-cm pieces

¼–⅓ cup red wine vinegar

1 lb 8 oz–2 lb 4 oz/675 g–1 kg ripe tomatoes, peeled, and chopped, juices reserved

1–2 tbsp sugar

salt and pepper

2 tbsp capers

1–2 tbsp toasted pine nuts

18 pitted green or black olives, chopped

1–2 tbsp chopped fresh basil

Eggplants were originally brought from North Africa to Spain. When the Jews fled Spain, Sicily, and Southern Italy during the Inquisition, they took their beloved eggplants with them. Caponata alla Guidea (Jewish-style) is served in Italy as a cold dish.

Using a swivel-bladed vegetable peeler, peel the eggplants (this is optional). Cut into 1-inch/2.5-cm cubes.

Heat about 4 tablespoons of oil in a large deep skillet over medium–high heat. Add the eggplants and cook for 5 minutes, or until brown on all sides, tossing and stirring; you may need to work in batches. Using a slotted spoon, remove to paper towels to drain.

Add the onion to the oil remaining in the skillet (add more oil if necessary) and cook for 5–7 minutes, or until softened and golden. Stir in the garlic and celery and cook for 1 minute.

Add the vinegar, tomatoes, sugar, and salt and pepper to taste. Simmer over medium heat for 15 minutes, or until the sauce is reduced and thickened, stirring frequently. Stir in the capers, pine nuts, and olives and cook for 2 minutes more.

Return the eggplant cubes to the skillet and simmer for 5 minutes to blend the flavors. Remove from the heat and stir in the basil. Leave to cool completely. Transfer to a serving dish and refrigerate, covered, for 4 hours or overnight. Serve cold.

desserts, cakes & cookies

Most people love desserts, cakes, and cookies, but Jews, perhaps because of their involvement in the early sugar trade, really love desserts. For Jews, these desserts represent joy and happiness and so are often associated with holidays and family celebrations.

Jewish desserts tend to be simple and homely, often based on fresh or dried fruit, like compotes or fresh fruit salads, as these desserts originated from agricultural festivals that celebrated the abundance of local fruit harvests. They are also popular with all Jewish communities because Jewish dietary laws forbid the mixing of meat and dairy foods in a meal.

When it comes to baking cakes and cookies, especially for the Sabbath and the holidays, Jews really excel, particularly at Passover when no flour or leavening agents are used. Many of these delicious specialities were adopted from their country of origin—German Jews made rich honey cakes and fine buttery cookies, New York-style cheesecakes originated from Russia and Poland, and the famous plavas, sponge cakes, and almond macaroons were originally found in the Sephardic communities of Spain and Morocco.

summer fruit compote

serves 8–10

20 minutes, plus 4 hours
30 minutes cooling & chilling

15–30 minutes

4 cups water
1 cinnamon stick
2–4 cloves
juice of 1 orange or lemon
sugar or artificial sweetener, to taste
6 peaches, skinned and sliced
6 nectarines or plums, sliced

6 ripe apricots, halved or quartered
2 1/2–3 cups sweet cherries,
   stoned if you like
3–6 cups mixed soft berries, such as
   strawberries, halved if large,
   raspberries and blueberries

cream, yogurt, or vanilla ice cream,
   to serve (optional)

Fruit compotes provide an ideal finish to a heavy meal and are characteristic of Ashkenazic cooking. Flavorings can include cinnamon, cloves, nutmeg, vanilla, orange, or lemon and various liqueurs.

Pour the water into a large wide pan (enough to just cover the first batch of fruit). Add the cinnamon stick, cloves, fruit juice, and sugar (start with the minimum amount and taste after all the fruit has been poached).

Bring to a boil over high heat and add the peaches. Reduce the heat to medium and simmer for 2–5 minutes, depending on their ripeness, until just tender.

Using a large skimmer or slotted spoon, gently transfer the peach slices to a large bowl, draining as much of the liquid against the side of the pan as possible.

Add the nectarines to the pan and cook as the peaches. Transfer to the bowl. Cook the apricots in the same way, then the cherries, adding to the bowl as they become tender; do not over-cook as the fruit continues to cook in the bowl. Add more water to the pan as necessary.

Stir in the soft berries and swirl gently, just to cover with the liquid. Simmer for 1 minute. Remove the berries to the bowl and taste the syrup. Adjust the sweetness. If the syrup is too thin, increase the heat and boil until slightly thickened and reduced. Pour over the fruit. Leave to cool, then refrigerate, covered, for 4 hours or overnight. Serve with heavy cream, yogurt, or vanilla ice cream, if you like.

matzo-apple pudding

 serves 6

20 minutes,
plus 10 minutes standing

55 minutes

4 matzos

12 no-soak dried apricots, chopped

3/4 cup dark or golden raisins

1/2 cup pitted dried dates, chopped

2/3 cup toasted almonds or pecan
nuts, chopped

1/2 cup sugar, plus extra for sprinkling

1 tsp ground cinnamon

1/2 tsp freshly grated nutmeg

grated zest and juice of 1 orange

3 eggs

3 tbsp fine matzo meal

4 oz/115 g pareve margarine, melted,
plus extra for greasing

2 dessert apples, peeled, cored, and
thinly sliced

2 tbsp apricot conserve

1 tbsp water

Apple pudding is the traditional Sabbath pudding. Made with noodles, it was eaten all year round in Russia and Poland, even made with oven-dried apple rings. Replacing noodles with matzos makes it an ideal Passover dessert.

Preheat the oven to 350°F/180°C. Break the matzos into small pieces into a large bowl. Cover with cold water. Leave to stand for 10 minutes, or until completely softened. Drain well, return to the bowl and beat with a fork until a batter-like consistency forms.

Add the dried fruit and nuts and mix to combine. Stir in half the sugar, the cinnamon, nutmeg, and orange zest and juice. Set aside.

Using an electric mixer, beat the eggs in a medium bowl with the remaining sugar for 5 minutes, or until thick and lightened and the sugar is completely dissolved. Add the matzo-fruit mixture, matzo meal, half the melted margarine and the sliced apples and gently fold into the eggs.

Pour into a deep greased baking dish, smoothing the top evenly. Drizzle the remaining melted margarine over the top and sprinkle with a little sugar. Bake for 50 minutes, or until puffed and golden-brown and a knife inserted in the center comes out clean.

Heat the apricot conserve in a small pan with the water. Brush over the top of the hot pudding and leave to cool slightly before serving.

lokshen pudding
(kugel) with dried fruit

serves 4–6

20 minutes

1 hour 10–20 minutes

2¹/2 cups milk
4 oz/115g dried vermicelli, or very thin spaghetti
2 large eggs
4 tbsp sugar
grated zest and juice of 1 orange or lemon
¹/4 tsp salt
¹/2 tsp cinnamon

¹/4 tsp freshly grated nutmeg
1–2 tsp vanilla extract
2 tbsp butter or margarine, melted, plus extra for greasing
1 cup no-soak dried apricots, chopped
1 cup dried cranberries and/or Morello cherries
¹/4 cup slivered almonds

Baked noodle puddings are a staple of Ashkenazic Jews. Because cooking was forbidden on the Sabbath, these dishes could be put in a very slow oven and baked all night. Kugels can be sweet or savory. This is delicious served with a fruit sauce or coulis.

Put the milk into a large pan and bring to a boil over medium–high heat. Add the pasta and cook over medium–low heat for 20–25 minutes, or until tender and most of the milk has been absorbed.

Preheat the oven to 350°F/180°C. Beat the eggs in a medium bowl with the sugar, orange zest and juice, salt, cinnamon, nutmeg, and vanilla extract until well blended.

Pour the melted butter into the egg mixture, add the dried fruit, and stir to combine. Add the cooked pasta and milk and toss to combine. Turn the mixture into a lightly greased baking or soufflé dish and sprinkle the top with the almonds.

Set the dish in a shallow roasting pan and pour in enough boiling water to come halfway up the side of the dish (this makes the texture of the pudding creamier). Cover the dish with foil. Bake for 25 minutes.

Remove the foil and bake for 15–20 minutes more, or until set and golden-brown and the almonds are well colored; a knife inserted into the center should come out clean. Leave to cool slightly before cutting into wedges, or serve at room temperature.

blood orange sorbet

serves 6–8

25 minutes, plus
7–8 hours 30 minutes freezing;
5–10 minutes softening

15 minutes

1½ cups freshly squeezed juice of
    blood oranges (from about 8–10
    medium-large oranges)
1 lemon
1¼ cups water

¾ cup sugar
1–2 tbsp Campari or orange liqueur
    (optional)
2 egg whites

*Granitas and water ices have been
particularly popular with Sephardic
Jews because they are so
refreshing in the hot climates of
Southern Europe, North Africa, and
India. As they do not contain milk
or cream, they can be served after
milk or meat meals.*

Using a swivel-bladed vegetable peeler, peel the zest from 2 of the oranges
and the lemon. Put into a medium pan with the water and sugar.

Bring to a boil over high heat, stirring until the sugar is dissolved, then
reduce the heat and simmer, without stirring, for 10 minutes. Remove from
the heat and leave to cool.

Squeeze the juice from all the oranges to make 12 fl oz/350ml juice, and
add to the syrup. Then stir in the juice from the lemon and Campari, if
using. Strain, or remove the strips of zest, and pour into a shallow plastic
freezerproof container. Freeze for 3–4 hours, or until frozen around the
edges.

Remove from the freezer. Using a knife, cut the frozen mixture into chunks
and put into a food processor. Process for 45 seconds, or until lightened
and slushy. Return the mixture to the container, spreading evenly, and
return to the freezer for 1½ hours.

In a small bowl using an electric mixer, beat the egg whites until they hold
their shape. Remove the orange mixture from the freezer, cut up again and
spoon into the food processor. Process for 45 seconds, then add the egg
whites and, using the pulse button, pulse until well blended. Return to the
container and freeze for at least 3 hours, or until firm. Soften for 5–10
minutes in the refrigerator before serving.

caramelized quinces

 serves 8–10

 15 minutes,
plus 30 minutes cooling

40–45 minutes

1 ¼ cups sugar, plus extra
  for sprinkling
1 cinnamon stick
peeled zest of 1 lemon
3 cups water
1–2 tsp vanilla extract

4 quinces, well washed
freshly squeezed juice from
  3–4 lemons
rosewater or orange flowerwater
  (optional)
sour cream or yogurt, to serve

*Spanish Jews fell in love with the
quinces of the Arabs in Andalusia
and soon quince paste, quince
preserves and quince jelly became
part of their culinary repertoire.
The quince cannot be eaten raw
and requires long cooking times,
but it is well worth the wait.*

Put the sugar, cinnamon stick, and lemon zest into a large stainless steel pan
and add the water. Bring to a boil over high heat, stirring occasionally, to
dissolve the sugar. Continue to boil for 5 minutes, or until slightly reduced.
Remove from the heat and leave to cool slightly. Stir in the vanilla extract.

Cut the quinces in half lengthwise and trim the ends. If you like, use a
melon baller or a teaspoon to remove the cores. Put the quinces into a
non-metallic bowl with the lemon juice as you prepare them to prevent
from discoloring.

Add the quinces and their lemon juice to the sugar syrup and cook,
covered, for 20–25 minutes, or until tender when pierced with a knife tip.
Meanwhile, preheat the oven to 450°F/230°C.

Transfer the poached quinces to a medium baking dish and pour over the
syrup. Sprinkle each quince with a little sugar.

Bake for 10 minutes, or until the sugar caramelizes, the top is golden-
brown, and the edges lightly charred. Remove to a heatproof surface and
leave to cool to room temperature. Sprinkle with rosewater, if using. Serve
with sour cream or yogurt.

exotic fruit salad

serves 6–8

20–25 minutes

10 minutes

1 large mango

1 papaya

3 persimmons

10 oz/280 g litchis, peeled and pitted

6 oz/175 g kumquats, halved

4 kiwi fruit, peeled and sliced
crosswise

4 ripe passion fruit

2 cups seedless red or green grapes,
halved if large

1 cup large dates, pitted and halved

syrup

2–3 tbsp honey

½ cup water

pared zest and juice of 1 lemon or
orange

4–6 fresh mint sprigs, plus extra
leaves to decorate

2 tsp vanilla extract

*For all Jews, fruit has been symbolic
of nature's bounty since biblical
times, but modern Israel has defied
nature and turned itself into a
major fruit-producing country. A
large selection of both dried and
fresh fruit is offered to visitors at
all times of the day.*

Prepare the syrup. Put the honey, water, lemon zest, and juice into a small
pan. Crush the mint sprigs to help release their flavor and add to the pan.
Bring to a boil over high heat, then reduce the heat and simmer for
5 minutes, or until reduced and slightly syrupy. Remove from the heat and
leave to cool slightly. Stir in the vanilla extract.

Using a sharp knife, cut down lengthwise either side of the long flat pit in
the mango. Cut any flesh from the stone and put into a large bowl. Peel
the skin from the mango halves and thinly slice the flesh. Put into the bowl.

Cut the pawpaw lengthways in half and scoop out and discard the black
pips. Peel the skin from each half and slice the flesh. Add to the mango in
the bowl. Remove the stem end from the persimmons and cut lengthwise
in half. Place cut-side down on a board and thinly slice. Add to the bowl.

Add the litchis, kumquat halves, and kiwi fruit slices to the bowl and strain
over the syrup. Toss gently to mix.

Cut the passion fruit in half and scoop out the flesh with the small black
seeds and add to the bowl. Sprinkle over the grapes and arrange the date
halves around the edge. Refrigerate, covered, until ready to serve.
Decorate with mint leaves.

dried fruit compote

serves 8

10 minutes, plus 3–4 hours
30 minutes cooling & chilling

20–25 minutes

1 lb/450 g pitted prunes

1 lb/450 g no-soak dried apricots

8 oz/225 g no-soak dried pears

8 oz/225 g no-soak dried
apple rings

1 cup raisins or golden raisins

2 tbsp honey or
sugar (optional)

grated zest and juice of 1 orange or
lemon

1 cinnamon stick

1 tbsp vanilla extract

2 tbsp toasted slivered almonds or
pine nuts, to decorate

*Eastern European Jews depended
on dried fruit as a source of
vitamins and minerals and to
enliven a fairly bland diet during
the long winter months. Dried fruit
is used in many Jewish cakes and
pastries, in fruit salads, and
compotes like this one.*

cook's tip

*The poaching liquid can be wine,
water, tea, or fruit juices. Serve the
compote with vanilla ice cream. It
is also delicious served with thick
natural yogurt for breakfast.*

Put the prunes, apricots, pears, apple rings, and raisins into a large pan and
pour in enough water to cover by 1 inch/2.5 cm.

Stir in the honey, if using, orange zest and juice, and cinnamon stick and
bring to a boil over high heat, skimming any foam that rises to the surface
of the fruit.

Simmer, partially covered, over low heat for 15 minutes, or until the dried
fruit is plump and tender. Remove the pan from the heat and stir in the
vanilla extract.

Remove the fruit to a heatproof serving bowl and, if you like, bring the
liquid to a boil and cook over medium–high heat until thickened and
syrupy. Pour over the fruit and leave to cool.

Refrigerate, covered, for 3–4 hours or overnight. To serve, sprinkle with the
toasted almonds or pine nuts and serve chilled.

lekach

makes 18–24 slices

25 minutes

50 minutes–1 hour

2½ cups all-purpose flour, plus extra for dusting

2 tsp baking powder

½ tsp bicarbonate of soda

¼ tsp salt

1 tsp ground cinnamon

¼ tsp ground cloves

2 eggs

1 cup sugar

½ cup vegetable oil, plus extra for oiling

¾ cup plus 2 tbsp good-quality dark honey

2 tbsp rum, brandy, or whisky

½ cup strong black coffee

grated zest of 1 orange

½ cup walnuts, pecans, or almonds, coarsely chopped

½ cup dark or golden raisins

½ cup stem ginger in syrup, chopped

confectioners' sugar for dusting

This spicy cake probably derives from the ancient German gingerbreads and became a festive cake for the Jews, to be served at all joyful occasions. Honey cake is highly traditional at Jewish New Year, the honey symbolizing the hope for a "sweet New Year."

Preheat the oven to 350°F/180°C. Oil two 9 × 5-inch/23 × 13-cm loaf pans and line the bases with nonstick baking parchment. Oil again. Sift the flour, baking powder, bicarbonate of soda, salt, cinnamon, and cloves together into a large bowl. Set aside.

Put the eggs and sugar into a separate large bowl. Using an electric mixer, beat for 3–5 minutes, or until pale and creamy. Gradually beat in the oil, honey, rum, coffee, and orange zest until blended and smooth.

Gradually beat the flour mixture into the egg mixture until a smooth batter forms. Put the nuts, raisins, and ginger into another bowl and toss with 1–2 tablespoons of flour. Stir into the batter.

Divide the batter evenly between the 2 loaf pans and smooth the surfaces evenly. Tap each gently against the work surface to release any air bubbles. Bake for 50 minutes–1 hour, or until a thin knife inserted in the center comes out with a few crumbs attached.

Leave to cool on a wire rack for 10 minutes. Run a sharp knife around the edges to loosen from the pans, then leave to cool completely. Turn out on to the rack, then turn right-side up. Dust with confectioners' sugar. Serve in slices.

cook's tip

Prepare the cake 2–3 days ahead to allow the flavors to develop.

liz's apple cake

serves 6–8

25 minutes

1 hour 15–30 minutes

1¾ cups self-rising flour
1 tsp cinnamon
1½ tsp baking powder
½ cup + 2 tbsp soft margarine, plus extra for greasing
generous ½ cup sugar, plus extra for sweetening (optional) and sprinkling
2 eggs, lightly beaten at room temperature

1 tsp vanilla essence
2 lb 4 oz /1kg (about 4 large)tart cooking apples, such as Bramleys, peeled, cored and thinly sliced
grated rind and juice of 1 lemon
flaked almonds, for sprinkling
extra-thick heavy cream, to serve (optional)

Apple cake is one of the standbys of Ashkenazic Jewish baking. Apple cake made with oil is a popular choice for Hanukkah (festival of lights) as the oil symbolizes the holiday's miracle. This recipe uses margarine and makes a light yet very moist cake.

cook's tip

If you like a sharp, strong apple flavor, do not sweeten the apples with sugar. You cannot test if the cake is done by inserting a knife into the center because the apples keep the mixture around them extra moist.

Preheat the oven to 325°F/160°C. Grease a 8-inch/20-cm loose-based deep cake pan and line the base with nonstick baking parchment. Grease again. Sift the flour, half the cinnamon, and baking powder into a bowl.

Put the soft margarine and sugar into a separate large bowl and, using an electric mixer, beat for 3 minutes, or until light and creamy. Very gradually beat in the beaten eggs; if the mixture begins to "separate," stir in a little of the flour mixture to bind it back together. Beat in the vanilla extract. Gently stir in the flour mixture until just blended.

In another nonmetallic bowl, toss the apples with the lemon zest and juice, the remaining cinnamon, and 1–2 tablespoons sugar, if using.

Spoon about one-third of the cake mixture into the tin and spread evenly. Add about half the apple slices in an even layer and spread another third of the mixture over the apples. Add the remaining apple slices and cake mixture in dollops, spreading evenly; it does not matter if they mix.

Sprinkle with the almonds and another tablespoon of sugar and bake for 1¼–1½ hours. Cover the top loosely with foil if it colors too quickly or reduce the oven temperature slightly. Transfer to a wire rack and leave to cool for 10 minutes. Run a sharp knife around the edge to loosen the cake from the side of the pan then remove the side. Leave to cool completely, but do not chill. Serve with a dollop of heavy cream, if you like.

luscious chocolate passover
roulade

serves 8–10

40 minutes,
plus 30 minutes cooling

15 minutes

pareve margarine, for greasing
7 oz/200 g bittersweet or very dark
  good-quality chocolate, chopped
4 tbsp strong black coffee, orange
  juice, or water
6 eggs, separated
4–6 tbsp sugar, or to taste

2 tsp vanilla extract
cocoa powder, for dusting
3/4–1 cup apricot or raspberry
  conserve
confectioners' sugar, for dusting

Chocolate cakes and desserts have been popular with Jews for centuries as they were involved with the cocoa trade and the first chocolate production in Amsterdam and other Sephardic Jewish centers.

Preheat the oven to 350°F/180°C. Grease a 15½ x 10½-inch/39 x 26-cm jelly roll pan and line with nonstick baking parchment. Grease the paper. Put the chocolate into a small pan with the coffee and heat gently over low heat until melted and smooth, stirring occasionally.

Put the egg yolks, half the sugar, and vanilla into a large mixing bowl. Using an electric mixer, beat for 5–7 minutes, or until pale and thick and the mixture leaves a "ribbon trail" when the beaters are lifted. Beat a spoonful of the mixture into the chocolate, then fold the chocolate mixture into the yolks.

Put the egg whites into a separate large bowl and, using cleaned beaters, beat until soft peaks form. Gradually beat in the remaining sugar in 3 batches, beating well after each addition, until stiff peaks form. Stir a spoonful of whites into the chocolate mixture, then fold in the remaining whites. Turn into the jelly roll pan, spreading evenly. Bake for 15 minutes, or until the cake springs back when lightly pressed with a finger.

Lay another sheet of parchment a little larger than the cake pan on a work surface. Dust with cocoa powder. Remove the cake to a wire rack, loosen the paper from the pan and invert on to the cocoa-lined paper. Peel off the paper from the cake and, beginning with one short edge, roll the cake and bottom paper up tightly together. Leave on a wire rack to cool.

When cold, unroll the cake. Spread the conserve to within 1 inch/2.5 cm of the edges and, using the paper as a guide, re-roll the cake without the paper. Dust with confectioners' sugar and transfer on to a serving plate.

cook's tip

Fill with whipped cream for a dairy dessert, or chestnut purée lightened with cream for a special occasion.

orange & lemon
passover plava

serves 6–8

30 minutes,
plus 30 minutes cooling

35–40 minutes

pareve margarine, for greasing
6 eggs, separated
generous 1 cup sugar
1/4 cup fine matzo meal
1 3/4 cup finely ground almonds or
  potato flour

grated zest and juice of 1 lemon and
  1 orange
1/2 tsp almond extract
slivered almonds, to decorate
4 cups confectioners' sugar

The plava sponge cake is one of the great Sephardic contributions not only to Jewish cuisine but also to gastronomy in general. The substitution of ground almonds or other nuts, or potato flour or matzo meal, for wheat flour yields a light delicate texture.

Preheat the oven to 350°F/180°C. Lightly grease a 9-inch/23-cm springform pan. Put the egg yolks into a large bowl with half the sugar and, using an electric mixer, beat for 5 minutes, or until the mixture is thick and pale and leaves a "ribbon trail" when the beaters are lifted.

Put the egg whites into a separate large bowl and, using cleaned beaters, beat until soft peaks form. Gradually beat in the remaining sugar in 3–4 batches, beating well after each addition, until soft and glossy.

Stir the matzo meal, ground almonds, and lemon and orange zest together in a bowl. Fold the matzo meal-almond mixture and egg whites alternately in 3 batches into the lightened egg yolk mixture. Fold in the almond extract. Pour into the springform pan. Sprinkle with the slivered almonds.

Bake for 35–40 minutes, or until puffed and golden-brown and the edges begin to pull away from the pan. Remove to a wire rack to cool for 5 minutes. Run a sharp knife around the edge of the pan, unclip the side of the pan and remove. Leave to cool completely.

Sift the confectioners' sugar into a medium bowl. Whisk in the lemon and orange juices until a smooth glaze forms. Spoon over the cake, allowing it to drip over the side. The cake is best served on the same day.

cheesecake

new york jewish-style

serves 10–12

25 minutes,
plus 8 hours chilling

50–55 minutes

12–14 graham crackers

½ tsp ground cinnamon

2–3 tbsp butter or margarine,
melted, plus extra for greasing

3 cups cream cheese, softened

6 oz/175g sugar

grated zest of 1 lemon or 1 orange

2 tsp vanilla extract

3 eggs

topping

1 cup sour cream

2 tbsp sugar

1 tsp vanilla extract

strawberries, halved, or raspberries,
to decorate (optional)

Now a New York deli staple, the cheesecake that Jews knew from Central and Eastern Europe probably evolved from the Russian Easter Pashka—a molded dessert with a curd cheese base enriched with butter, sour cream, eggs, sugar, and candied fruit.

cook's tip

As the cheesecake cools after baking the topping, run a sharp knife around the edge to separate the cake from the pan to help prevent it from splitting.

Preheat the oven to 350°F/180°C. Lightly grease a 9-inch/23-cm springform pan. Break the crackers into a food processor and process until fine crumbs form. Add the cinnamon and butter and process to mix well. Turn into the pan. Press the crumbs on to the base and about 1½ inches/ 4 cm up the side. Bake for 5 minutes to set, then remove to a wire rack.

Put the cream cheese into a bowl and, using an electric mixer, beat to soften. Add the sugar and continue beating until smooth. Add the lemon zest and vanilla extract, then beat in the eggs, one at a time, until smooth. Pour into the baked case.

Bake for 40–45 minutes, or until firm around the edge but slightly wobbly in the center. If it begins to brown, reduce the heat. Remove to a wire rack.

Increase the oven temperature to 425°F/220°C. Prepare the topping. Beat the ingredients together in a small bowl. Pour over the baked cheesecake, tilting the cake slightly to spread evenly. Bake for 5 minutes, then remove to a wire rack to cool. Refrigerate overnight.

To serve, run a sharp knife around the edge of the pan to loosen, then unclip and gently remove the side. Slide the cake on to a serving plate. Arrange strawberry halves or raspberries around the edge, if you like.

rum-raisin rice pudding

serves 6

15 minutes, plus 4 hours
30 minutes soaking & chilling

55 minutes

salt
3/4 cup risotto rice, such as Arborio,
    or pudding rice
3 cups milk
2 vanilla beans, split

1/2 cup sugar, plus extra
    for sprinkling
3/4 cup raisins, soaked in
    1/3 cup rum
2 egg yolks

Rice pudding is a traditional and favorite dessert in all Jewish communities. In the Sephardic world, Spanish versions are flavored with vanilla or cinnamon. Some Arab versions are fragrant with rosewater, and saffron, and cardamom is used in Iran.

Bring a medium pan of salted water to a boil over high heat. Add the rice and simmer over low heat for 5 minutes, or until just beginning to soften. Drain.

In a separate pan, bring the milk to a simmer. Add the rice and the vanilla beans and simmer for 25 minutes, or until the rice is tender; there will be a lot of milky liquid left. Add the sugar and the raisins and their soaking liquid and cook for 5 minutes, or until the sugar is dissolved. Remove from the heat.

Preheat the oven to 350°F/180°C. Beat the egg yolks in a small bowl, then beat in some of the hot rice mixture. Stir the egg mixture into the pan.

Pour the mixture into a lightly greased baking dish and bake for 15 minutes, or until just set but still soft.

Sprinkle the top of the pudding evenly with sugar and cook under a preheated hot broiler, close to the heat, for 1–2 minutes, or until the sugar caramelizes. Leave to cool to room temperature, then serve. Alternatively, refrigerate, covered, for 4 hours and serve chilled.

almond macaroons

makes 16–18 cookies

20 minutes

10–12 minutes

2 cups ground almonds
scant ³/4 cup sugar
1 egg white
¹/4 tsp almond extract

Almond macaroons are a Passover specialty that contain almonds, sugar, and egg whites. As such, they also provide an ideal neutral sweet to follow any meal—meat or dairy. These macaroons are quick and easy to make.

cook's tip

Ground almonds are available in packets, but if you start with whole blanched almonds, they have a much better flavor. Simply grind them very finely in a food processor, but do not over-process or they will form a paste.

Preheat the oven to 350°F/180°C. Put the ground almonds and sugar into a medium bowl.

Using a whisk or fork, beat the egg white and almond extract in a small bowl until frothy and beginning to hold its shape. Gradually beat into the ground almond mixture until the mixture becomes a fairly stiff paste. You may not need all the egg white; do not make the mixture too soft.

Drop tablespoonfuls of the mixture into mini baking cases and arrange on a baking sheet, or roll tablespoonfuls into balls and drop into the paper cases. Flatten the mixture or balls with a fork dipped in water. Alternatively, drop tablespoonfuls of the mixture 1-inch/2.5-cm apart on to a baking sheet lined with a non-stick liner or baking parchment.

Bake for 10–12 minutes, or until just set but still soft inside. Do not allow the macaroons to brown; they should be very pale. Transfer to a wire rack and leave to cool until firm before removing from the baking sheet. Leave to cool completely. Store in an airtight container.

maamoul date-filled cookies

makes about 24 cookies

30 minutes

20–25 minutes

dough
6 oz/175g all-purpose flour
2 tbsp sugar
3 oz/85 g unsalted butter or
  margarine, plus extra for greasing
1 tbsp rosewater or orange
  flowerwater

2–3 tbsp milk
confectioners' sugar, for dusting

date filling
2/3 cup pitted dried dates, chopped
1–2 tsp rosewater or orange
  flowerwater

These divine cookies are a specialty of Sephardic Jews from Southern Europe to Northern Africa. The most refined ones are found in Morocco. The fillings vary, from walnuts to pistachios, to the dates featured here.

Preheat the oven to 325°F/160°C. Lightly grease a large baking sheet. Prepare the filling. Put the dates into a food processor with the rosewater and process to blend. With the machine running, add a tablespoon or two of boiling water, just enough to make a soft paste. Scrape into a bowl and set aside to cool.

Prepare the dough. Sift the flour into a large bowl and stir in the sugar. Cut the butter into small pieces and add to the flour, rubbing in with your fingers until fine crumbs form. Sprinkle over the rosewater and 2 tablespoons of the milk. Toss and mix gently until a soft dough forms. Add a little more milk if necessary, but do not allow the dough to become sticky. Form into a ball, pull off small pieces and roll into 1-inch/2.5-cm balls.

Press into the center of each ball with your finger and rotate to create a well. Add a little filling. Pinch the open edges of the dough together to seal.

Arrange the filled balls seam-side down on the baking sheet 1-inch/2.5-cm apart. Press the balls into long shapes and use tweezers to pinch the tops 3 times. Bake for 20–25 minutes, or until just set. Do not allow them to brown; they should be soft and pale.

Transfer to a wire rack to cool for 10 minutes. Lightly dust with confectioners' sugar, covering completely. Dust again when completely cool. Shake gently to remove any excess, then store in a single layer in an airtight container.

teiglach—honey-poached
pastry nuggets

makes about 35 nuggets

**25 minutes, plus
30 minutes chilling**

I hour 30 minutes

dough
2½ cups all-purpose flour, plus extra
if necessary
½ tsp baking powder
½ tsp ground ginger
¼ tsp salt
3 eggs, plus 2 egg yolks
2 tbsp vegetable oil, plus extra for
oiling

scant to generous I cup chopped
walnuts and/or sesame seeds, for
rolling

syrup
I ½ cups good-quality fragrant honey
grated zest of I lemon (optional)
I tsp ground ginger

*These "little pieces of dough" are a
popular Ashkenazic sweetmeat,
eaten at Rosh Hashanah (Jewish
New Year). Traditionally, these
dough balls were piled in pyramids,
using the sticky syrup as a kind of
glue. They are still displayed in
Jewish bakeries at the New Year.*

cook's tip

*Some people bake the dough
pieces in a 350°F/180°C oven
before poaching in the syrup.
However, this makes the pastry
much more firm. Store
in a single layer in an
airtight container.*

Prepare the dough. Sift the flour, baking powder, ginger, and salt into a large
bowl and stir to blend. Make a well in the center. Beat the eggs, egg yolks,
and oil together in a small bowl and pour into the well. Gradually stir the
flour mixture into the egg mixture until a sticky dough forms. Turn out on
to a lightly floured work surface and knead until smooth and just slightly
elastic, adding a little more flour if the dough is too sticky. Shape into a ball
and refrigerate, tightly wrapped, for 30 minutes.

Meanwhile, prepare the syrup. Bring the ingredients to a boil in a large
deep pan (to prevent boiling over).

Cut the dough into 6–8 pieces and, on a lightly floured work surface, roll
each piece into long thin sausage shapes about ½-inch/1-cm thick. Using a
knife dipped in flour, cut into ½-inch/1-cm pieces.

Lightly oil 2 pieces of foil and lay on the surface. Working in batches, add
the dough pieces to the honey syrup, and simmer for 15 minutes or until
a rich golden in color and cooked through. (If the honey thickens too
much, add a little water to thin.) Repeat with all the dough pieces.

Put the walnuts and sesame seeds, if using, into separate shallow dishes.
Using a slotted spoon, remove the teiglach and turn into the nuts and/or
sesame seeds, rolling them with a kitchen fork to coat. Arrange on the foil.

raspberry
almond rugalach

makes about 32 cookies

30 minutes,
plus 2 hours chilling

40 minutes–1 hour

cream cheese pastry
2²/3 cups all-purpose flour
¹/2 tsp salt
¹/2 tsp baking powder
1 tbsp sugar
8 oz/225 g unsalted butter, softened
1 cup cream cheese, softened
5 tbsp sour cream
¹/2 tsp almond extract

milk, for glazing
slivered almonds, for sprinkling

filling
1 cup raspberry conserve
¹/2 tsp almond extract
³/4 cup chopped or slivered almonds

These crescent-shaped pastry-like cookies are one of the most popular Jewish cookies in the US. Rugalach means "horn-shaped" in Yiddish, although they are formed like mini croissants. Fillings vary from the traditional cinnamon-nut to chocolate, apricot, and raspberry.

Sift the flour, salt, baking powder, and sugar into a medium bowl. Using an electric mixer, beat the butter and cream cheese together until smooth and light. Beat in the sour cream and almond extract. Stir in the flour mixture to form a soft dough. Shape into a ball and flatten. Wrap tightly and refrigerate for 2 hours, or until firm.

Preheat the oven to 350°F/180°C. Lightly grease 2 large baking sheets. Prepare the filling. Combine the conserve and almond extract in a small bowl. Cut the dough into 4 pieces. Roll out one piece at a time (keep remaining refrigerated) on a lightly floured work surface to ⅛ inch/3 mm thick. Cut into a 10-inch/25-cm circle using a plate as a template.

Spread the round with a quarter of the filling to within 1 inch/2.5 cm of the edge. Sprinkle with a quarter of the almonds. Cut into 8 equal wedges.

Starting at the outside edge, roll up each wedge to a crescent shape. Place on a baking sheet 2.5-cm/1-inch apart point-side down. Pull the ends down to form a crescent. Brush with milk and sprinkle with slivered almonds. Refrigerate while continuing with the remaining dough and filling. Bake, in batches, for 20 minutes, or until golden. Cool on a wire rack.

hamantaschen

makes about 24 cookies

35–40 minutes,
plus 2–3 hours chilling

20–27 minutes

cookie dough

5 oz/140 g plus 1 tbsp butter or
    margarine, plus extra for greasing
4 tbsp sugar
1 tsp vanilla extract
1 egg yolk
2–3 tbsp milk
2 cups all-purpose flour, plus extra
    for dusting
1 tsp baking powder
1/2 tsp salt
1 egg, beaten, for glazing

poppy seed filling

1 cup poppy seeds
1/2 cup milk
2 tbsp honey
4 tbsp sugar
3/4 cup raisins
1 tbsp butter
grated zest of 1 lemon and
    1 tbsp of juice

*This three-cornered cookie
celebrates the demise of Haman,
who decreed death for all Jews.
Ashkenazic Jews say the triangular
shape resembles Haman's hat;
others say that they are eating
the "poppy seed pockets"—
the pockets that he stuffed
with bribe money.*

Prepare the dough. Using an electric mixer, beat the butter with the sugar for 3–5 minutes, or until pale and creamy. Add the vanilla, egg yolk, and milk and beat until smooth. Sift in the flour, baking powder, and salt and stir until well blended. Turn out on to a floured work surface and knead lightly. Shape into a ball, flatten, and wrap tightly. Refrigerate for 2–3 hours.

Preheat the oven to 375°F/190°C. Lightly grease 2 large baking sheets. Prepare the filling. Put the poppy seeds, milk, honey, sugar, raisins, and butter into a medium pan. Simmer over medium heat for 5 minutes, or until thickened to a soft paste, stirring frequently to prevent sticking. Remove from the heat. Stir in the lemon zest and juice.

Cut the dough in half and refrigerate one half. Roll out the other half on a lightly floured work surface to 1/8 inch/3 mm thick. Cut out circles with a 2- or 3-inch/5- or 7.5-cm round cutter, re-rolling the trimmings to cut more.

Brush the edges with water. Put 1 teaspoon of filling in the center of each round and flatten slightly. Pinch the pastry at 3 evenly spaced intervals around the edge and pull toward the center to form a triangle with a little filling showing. Place the triangles on the baking sheets 1 inch/2.5 cm apart. Repeat with the remaining dough and filling. Brush with egg. Bake for 15–17 minutes, or until crisp and golden. Transfer to a wire rack to cool.

mandelbrodt

almond bread

makes about 36 slices

25 minutes

45 minutes

4 cups all-purpose flour

2 tsp baking powder

1/2 tsp salt

3 eggs

generous 1 cup sugar

1/2 cup vegetable oil, plus extra
  for oiling

grated zest of 1 lemon and
  1 tbsp of juice

1/2 tsp almond extract

3/4 cup coarsely chopped, split
  blanched or slivered almonds

*Mandelbrodt probably came to
Italy as biscotti alla Mandorla
via the Spanish Jews, although the
Germans and Dutch have their
own versions. They are ideal for
dunking into coffee or tea, or
dipping into sweet dessert wine.*

Preheat the oven to 350°F/180°C. Oil a large baking sheet. Sift the flour,
baking powder, and salt into a medium bowl.

Using an electric mixer, beat the eggs and sugar together for 3–5 minutes,
or until pale and creamy. Gradually beat in the oil, lemon zest and juice,
and the almond extract. Slowly beat in the flour mixture and the almonds
on low speed until the dough is well blended. Turn out on to a lightly
floured work surface and knead lightly.

Divide the dough in half and shape each half into 2 long flat loaves about
3 inches/7.5 cm wide and 1 1/2 inches/4 cm high. Transfer to the baking
sheets and bake for 35 minutes, or until golden-brown and set.

Transfer to a wire rack to cool slightly. Slide the loaves on to a cutting
board and, using a sharp or serrated knife, carefully cut into 3/4-inch/2-cm
slices; the dough will be slightly soft inside. Transfer the slices to 2 clean
greased baking sheets.

Bake the slices for 5 minutes on each side, or until crisp and golden-brown.
Transfer to a wire rack to cool. Store in an airtight container.

the best coconut
macaroons

makes 28–30 cookies

20 minutes

20 minutes

4 egg whites
1/4 tsp cream of tartar
generous 1 cup sugar
2 tsp freshly squeezed lemon juice

2 tsp vanilla extract
2 1/2 cups unsweetened shredded coconut

The entire Jewish community enjoys macaroons of all kinds at Passover. They are easy to make and have a wonderful chewy texture beneath a pale crisp exterior. The easiest, and best, of all macaroons are these coconut ones.

cook's tip

Shredded coconut is available in large supermarkets and specialist stores, unsweetened and sweetened, and gives a moist texture and real coconut flavor.

Preheat the oven to 300°F/150°C. Line 2 large baking sheets with nonstick baking parchment. Put the egg whites into a large bowl and, using an electric mixer, beat at medium speed until just frothy.

Add the cream of tartar and continue beating at high speed until firm peaks form. Gradually add the sugar, 2 tablespoons at a time, beating well after each addition, until the whites are stiff and glossy.

Sprinkle over the lemon juice, vanilla extract and shredded coconut and gently fold into the whites until just blended. Drop the mixture by tablespoonfuls 1 inch/2.5 cm apart on to the baking sheets to form pyramid shapes.

Bake for 20 minutes, or until golden-brown; they will still be soft in the center. Remove to a wire rack for 1–2 minutes to set, then slide the paper on to the rack and leave to cool for 5–7 minutes. Carefully peel the macaroons off the paper and leave to cool completely.

cinnamon balls

makes about 20 balls

25 minutes

10–12 minutes

2¹/2 cups ground almonds
³/4 cup castor sugar
1 tbsp ground cinnamon
2 egg whites

¹/8 tsp cream of tartar
1¹/4–1¹/2 cups confectioners' sugar

These are some of the easiest and most popular Passover cookies for American and British Jews. Because they contain no butter, they can follow a meat meal and, like many Passover cookies, they use ground nuts instead of flour which gives them a soft texture inside.

Preheat the oven to 325°F/160°C. Lightly grease 2 medium or 1 large baking sheet. Combine the ground almonds, about half the castor sugar, and the cinnamon in a medium bowl until evenly mixed.

Put the egg whites into a medium bowl and, using an electric mixer, beat at medium speed until just frothy. Add the cream of tartar and continue beating at high speed until firm peaks form.

Gradually add the remaining castor sugar, 2 tablespoons at a time, beating well after each addition, until the whites are stiff and glossy. Gently fold in the almond-sugar mixture.

Using wet hands to help prevent sticking, shape the mixture into walnut-size balls. Place about 1 inch/2.5 cm apart on the baking sheet or sheets. Bake for 10–12 minutes, or until golden-brown and set; do not overcook or they will be dry. Transfer to a wire rack to cool slightly.

Put the confectioners' sugar into a small deep bowl and roll each warm cinnamon ball in the sugar, turning to coat. Use a fork to lift out of the sugar, tap gently to remove the excess and transfer to the wire rack to cool completely. Add more confectioners' sugar if necessary. When cold, roll each ball in the sugar again. Store in an airtight container.

chocolate pecan torte

serves 18

25 minutes

35–40 minutes

7 oz/200 g bittersweet or best
  quality dark chocolate, chopped

5 oz/140 g unsalted butter or pareve
  margarine, plus extra for greasing

4 eggs

6 tbsp sugar

2 tsp vanilla extract

1 cup ground pecan nuts

1–2 tsp ground cinnamon

24 perfect pecan halves, toasted,
  to decorate

chocolate honey glaze

4 oz/115 g bittersweet or best
  quality dark chocolate, chopped

2 oz/55 g unsalted butter or pareve
  margarine

2 tbsp honey

½ tsp ground cinnamon

*It is probably no accident that Jews
love chocolate. Good-quality dark
chocolate is pareve—it contains no
milk or cream, so it can be used in
cakes, mousses, and pastries and
still be neutral, as long as no butter
or cream is used.*

Preheat the oven to 350°F/180°C. Lightly grease a 8 × 2½-inch/20 × 6-
cm springform pan. Line the base with nonstick baking parchment. Use
2 layers of foil to wrap the base and side of the pan.

Put the chocolate and butter into a heatproof bowl. Set over a pan of just
simmering water and heat until melted and smooth, stirring frequently.
Remove from the heat. Put the eggs, sugar, and vanilla extract into a large
bowl and, using an electric mixer, beat for 1–2 minutes, or until light and
foamy. On low speed, gradually beat in the chocolate mixture, then stir in
the ground nuts and cinnamon. Pour into the pan.

Set the filled pan in a roasting pan and pour in enough boiling water to
come halfway up the side. Bake for 25–30 minutes, or until puffed and the
edge is set but the center is still wobbly. Remove the cake pan from the
roasting pan and remove the foil. Cool on a wire rack.

Prepare the glaze. Put the ingredients into a heatproof bowl. Set over a
pan of simmering water. Stir until melted and smooth. Remove from the
heat. Dip in the pecan halves and place on baking parchment. Release the
cake from the pan. Pour over the glaze, spreading with a metal palette knife
and smoothing the side. Arrange the pecans around the edge. Leave to set.

fresh fruit kuchen

serves 8–12

25 minutes

35–40 minutes

cake

2²/₃ cups self-raising flour, plus extra
  for dusting
1 tsp baking powder
generous 1 cup sugar
6 oz/175 g unsalted butter or
  margarine, softened, plus extra
  for greasing
2 eggs, lightly beaten
½ cup milk
1 tsp vanilla extract

topping

5–6 large nectarines, peaches
  (skinned), or dessert apples, sliced,
  or 1 lb 8 oz/675 g large pitted
  cherries, halved
3 tbsp soft light brown sugar
1 tbsp ground cinnamon

*Rich buttery cakes, often baked
with fresh seasonal fruit, were
brought to America by German
Ashkenazic Jews during several
large waves of immigration. Many
cities have their German
settlements, where
German bakeries and
pastry shops abound.*

Preheat the oven to 375°F/190°C. Lightly grease a 9 x 9 x 2-inch/23 x 23 x 5-cm square cake pan. Line the base with nonstick baking parchment and grease again. Dust lightly with flour.

Prepare the cake. Sift the flour and baking powder into a large bowl, and stir in the sugar. Add the butter, eggs, milk, and vanilla, and using an electric mixer, beat on medium speed until smooth and well blended. Pour into the pan, spreading evenly.

Prepare the topping. Arrange the sliced fruit, overlapping or closely together, in rows on top of the cake mixture, pushing slightly into the batter. Mix the brown sugar and cinnamon together in a small bowl and sprinkle over the cake and fruit.

Bake for 35–40 minutes, or until the cake is golden-brown and set and begins to pull away from the edge.

Remove to a wire rack to cool for 3 minutes, or until set. Using the baking parchment as a guide, carefully lift out the cake on to the rack so that the fruit is facing upward. Leave to cool until just warm or room temperature and cut into squares.

spanish almond cake
with orange syrup

serves 12–14

30 minutes,
plus 8 hours soaking

1 hour

cake
butter or pareve margarine, for greasing

flour, for dusting

8 eggs, separated

1 cup sugar

grated zest of 2 oranges, juice reserved

2 tsp ground cinnamon

1/4 tsp ground cloves

1 cup ground almonds

3/4 cup blanched almonds, finely chopped

1 tsp vanilla extract

1/2 tsp almond extract

1/4 tsp cream of tartar

syrup
reserved orange juice plus extra to make 2 1/2 cups

1 cup sugar

orange segments, to serve (optional)

The ancient Spanish-Jewish community has a gastronomic repertoire of refined and delicious cakes, many flavored with oranges. Jews became specialists and merchants in the orange trade, introducing the fruit to Northern European cities.

cook's tip

After drizzling over the cake, the orange syrup will soak through and the cake will "float" in the syrup. Spoon over the excess syrup once or twice. Serve the cake with orange segments, if you like.

Preheat the oven to 350°F/180°C. Grease a 10-inch/25-cm cake pan. Line the base with baking parchment and grease again. Dust with flour.

Put the egg yolks into a large bowl with three-quarters of the sugar, orange zest, cinnamon, and cloves and, using an electric mixer, beat for 2 minutes, or until thick and pale. Beat in the almonds and extracts.

Put the egg whites into a separate large bowl and, using cleaned beaters, beat on medium speed until frothy. Add the cream of tartar and beat on high speed until soft peaks form. Add the remaining sugar in 2–3 batches, beating well after each addition, until stiff and glossy. Beat a spoonful of whites into the egg yolk mixture, then fold in the remaining whites. Spoon the mixture into the pan.

Bake for 1 hour, or until golden and set and the edges begin to pull away from the pan. Transfer to a wire rack. Pierce all over with a skewer. Turn out, remove the paper and return to the pan. Place on the rack set over a tray.

Bring the orange juice and sugar to a boil in a medium pan, stirring. Boil for 5 minutes, skimming any foam that rises to the surface. Leave to cool slightly. Drizzle over the cake and leave to be absorbed overnight.

cinnamon streusel
coffeecake

serves 10–12

30 minutes

50–55 minutes

streusel
1 cup pecans or walnuts, chopped
1–2 tsp ground cinnamon
3–4 tbsp sugar

cake
scant 1 cup all-purpose flour
1½ tsp baking powder
½ tsp bicarbonate of soda

4 oz/115 g unsalted butter or
margarine, softened, plus extra
for greasing
½ cup sugar
3 eggs, lightly beaten, at room
temperature
12 fl oz/350 ml sour cream
1 tsp vanilla extract
confectioners' sugar, for dusting

This type of cake, eaten with coffee rather than coffee-flavored, was one of the many German or Austrian specialties brought to America by Jews, along with strudel, rugelach, and meringues.

Preheat the oven to 350°F/180°C. Grease a 10-inch/25-cm fluted cake pan. Combine the streusel ingredients in a small bowl. Sift the flour, baking powder and bicarbonate of soda into a medium bowl.

Put the butter and sugar into a large bowl and, using an electric mixer, beat on low speed until combined. Continue beating on medium speed for 2 minutes, or until pale and fluffy. Gradually add the beaten eggs, about a tablespoon at a time, beating until smooth.

Beat in the flour mixture and sour cream, alternately in 3 batches on low speed until combined, then beat in the vanilla; do not over-beat.

Spoon a little over one-third of the batter into the pan, tilting to distribute evenly. Sprinkle with half the streusel mixture. Drop about one-third more of the batter by tablespoonfuls over the streusel mixture, carefully spreading to just cover. Sprinkle with the remaining streusel mixture. Drop the remaining batter over, spreading to just cover the streusel mixture. Tap the pan gently to knock out any air bubbles and even the mixture.

Bake for 50–55 minutes, or until puffed and golden and a fine knife inserted comes out clean. Remove to a wire rack. Leave to cool for 5–7 minutes. Run a knife around the edge of the pan and carefully ease the cake on to the rack. Serve at room temperature, dusted with confectioners' sugar.

breads & pastries

Nowadays, bread is a kind of fashion accessory with all kinds of ethnic loaves found in upmarket bread shops, delis, and supermarkets. Jewish bakeries produce fantastic traditional loaves as well as bagels, pastries, and coffeecakes so there is little need to bake these at home. But breads and pastries are important and symbolic in Jewish history, and so a little home baking reminds us of the tremendous significance of yeast and flour.

In addition to its historical and religious significance, bread has been a main source of sustenance for the Jewish people since biblical times. Ashkenazic Jews survived on dark, dense, heavy-textured breads, while Sephardic Jews used flat breads and pita breads for nourishment, as well as a vehicle for other ingredients. More recently, breads like pumpernickel and rye have become associated with deli sandwiches and filled pitas are available in sandwich bars, while challah is always enjoyed on the Sabbath.

Jewish baked goods often reflect the diverse countries of origin of the members of the Jewish communities, and pastries are no exception, with strudels from Austria and Hungary, fruit tarts from France, and baklava and other phyllo pastries from the Middle East and North Africa.

challah

makes 2 loaves

30–40 minutes, plus
10 hours standing and proving

40 minutes

2 ½ tsp easy-blend dried yeast

2 tbsp sugar

1 cup lukewarm water

5 ½ cups all-purpose flour, plus extra
for sprinkling

1 tsp salt

6 tbsp light vegetable oil, plus extra
for oiling

2 whole eggs and 1 egg yolk, lightly
beaten, plus 1 egg beaten with
¼ tsp salt, for glazing

sesame and poppy seeds,
for sprinkling

*Challah is made in a variety of
symbolic forms. The strands of long
plaited loaves symbolize love, round
loaves with "no beginning and no
end," baked for Rosh Hashanah,
symbolize continuity of life, while
sweet challahs are baked during
festivals to bring happiness.*

Put the yeast and half the sugar into the large bowl of a standard electric
mixer fitted with a dough hook, or into a large mixing bowl if kneading by
hand. Stir in the water and sprinkle in a little flour. Cover with a tea towel
and leave for 10 minutes, or until the mixture begins to bubble and foam.
Gradually beat in the remaining sugar, salt, oil, and eggs on low speed.

Gradually add the remaining flour until a sticky dough forms. Knead on
medium speed until the dough forms a ball around the hook, or knead by
hand. If still sticky, add a little more flour and continue to knead a little
longer. Remember that the dough should be soft, not firm.

Oil a large bowl and add the dough, turning to coat with the oil. Cover
with the tea towel and leave to rise in a warm place for 1–2 hours, or until
doubled in volume. Turn out on to a lightly floured work surface and knead
lightly to deflate. Return to the bowl, cover with plastic wrap and leave to
rise slowly overnight. This gives a much better texture.

Preheat the oven to 375°F/190°C. Lightly grease a large baking sheet. Turn
the dough out on to a lightly floured work surface and knead gently. Shape
into a ball and divide into 2 pieces. Working with one piece of dough at a
time, cut into 3 equal pieces and roll into 3 ropes about 18 inches/46 cm
long and 1 ½ inches/4 cm in diameter. Plait together and place on one side
of the baking sheet. Tuck the ends under each end of the loaf. Repeat with
the other piece of dough. Cover with the dish towel and leave to rise for
1 hour, or until doubled in size.

Brush each loaf with the egg mixture. Sprinkle one with sesame seeds and
one with poppy seeds. Bake for 40 minutes, or until a rich deep brown and
sounding hollow when tapped on the bottom. Cool on a wire rack.

cook's tip

*If you do not have an electric
mixer, you can use a food
processor instead.*

sesame pita breads

makes about 12 breads

20 minutes. plus 2 hours 45 minutes standing and proving

10–12 minutes

1 tbsp easy-blend dried yeast
1 tsp sugar
1 cup warm water
3½ cups plain or strong bread flour, or substitute 1 cup whole wheat flour for the same quantity of white, plus extra for sprinkling and dusting

1 tsp salt
vegetable oil, for oiling
½ cup sesame seeds

Pita bread, baked fresh all over Israel and the Middle East, is pressed flat and baked at high temperature to help create the "pocket" as it cools. Soft yet crusty, it has become very popular with the influence of Greek, Indian, and Middle Eastern food.

Combine the yeast, sugar and one-third of the water and stir for 1–2 minutes, or until dissolved. Sprinkle with a little flour and leave to stand, covered with a dish towel, for 5–7 minutes, or until the mixture begins to bubble. Put the remaining flour and salt into a food processor and, using the pulse button, process to blend. Stir the remaining warm water into the yeast mixture and, with the machine running, gradually pour into the flour, until a smooth dough ball forms. If it looks too dry, add a little more water.

Lightly oil a large bowl and add the dough, turning to coat on all sides to prevent a crust from forming. Cover with the dish towel and leave in a warm place to rise for 1½–2 hours, or until doubled in volume.

Turn the dough out on to a lightly floured work surface and knead lightly to deflate. Divide the dough into 12 equal-size pieces and roll each into a smooth ball. Transfer to a floured baking sheet and cover with the dish towel. Leave to rise for 30 minutes, or until doubled in volume.

Meanwhile, preheat the oven to 475°F/240°C. Flour 2 large baking sheets. Put the sesame seeds into a small bowl and roll each ball in the seeds to coat well. On a lightly floured work surface, roll each ball to a 5–6-inch/13–15-cm round or oval.

Transfer 3 or 4 dough rounds or ovals to each baking sheet. Bake for 3 minutes, or until just browned. Using kitchen tongs, turn and bake for 2–3 minutes, or until puffed and lightly browned. Continue with the remaining dough rounds or ovals. Transfer to a wire rack. Serve immediately.

bagels

makes 12 bagels

25 minutes, plus 2 hours 30 minutes standing and proving

40–50 minutes

1 tbsp easy-blend dried yeast
2 tbsp sugar
3 1/2 tbsp vegetable oil, plus extra for oiling
1 tsp salt
1 cup warm water

3 1/2 cups strong or all-purpose flour, plus extra if necessary and for dusting
1 egg, beaten, plus 1 egg beaten with 1/4 tsp salt, for glazing
poppy and sesame seeds, for sprinkling

Sold by street vendors in the Polish ghetto, bagels came to the US, Britain and Europe when the Jews left Eastern Europe. Bagels were sold from handcarts on New York's Lower East Side and in London's East End, becoming mainstream in the 1950s in New York.

Combine the yeast and half the sugar in a small bowl. Heat the remaining sugar, oil, salt, and water in a small pan for 1–2 minutes, or until warm and the sugar has dissolved, stirring. Pour into the yeast mixture. Cover with a dish towel and leave to stand for 5–7 minutes, or until the mixture begins to bubble. Put the flour into a food processor and, with the machine running, pour in the yeast mixture, then add the egg and process until a ball of dough forms. Add a little more flour if the dough is sticky; it should be smooth and elastic.

Lightly oil a large bowl and add the ball of dough, turning to coat on all sides to prevent a crust from forming. Cover with the dish towel and leave to rise in a warm place for 1 1/2–2 hours, or until doubled in volume. Turn out on to a lightly floured work surface. Knead lightly to deflate.

Divide the dough into 12 equal-size pieces. Roll each into a rope about 7 inches/18 cm long and shape into a ring. Wet one end and press firmly to seal. Arrange on a floured baking sheet, cover with the dish towel and leave to rise for 25 minutes, or until doubled in volume.

Meanwhile, preheat the oven to 400°F/200°C. Lightly oil 2 large baking sheets. Bring a large pan of water to a boil. Working in batches, slide a few bagels into the water and cook for 1 minute. Remove to paper towels to drain. Arrange the bagels on the baking sheets and carefully brush with the egg mixture. Sprinkle half with sesame seeds and the remainder with poppy seeds. Bake for 12–15 minutes, or until golden and shiny. Remove to a wire rack to cool slightly.

Serve warm with a variety of fillings, such as salmon and cream cheese.

rye bread

makes 2 loaves

**25–30 minutes, plus
2–4 hours 30 minutes proving**

35 minutes

1 tbsp easy-blend dried yeast

2½ cups warm water

2 tbsp sugar

2 tbsp vegetable oil, plus extra
for oiling

2¼ cups rye flour

3½ cups all-purpose flour, plus extra
as necessary and for dusting

2 tsp salt

2 tbsp caraway seeds, lightly crushed,
plus extra seeds for sprinkling

1 egg, lightly beaten, for glazing

A light rye bread, speckled with caraway seeds, is one of the most popular Jewish breads. It probably has its origins in the dark, strong-tasting, chewy breads from Russia and the slightly sour German pumpernickel. This is the traditional choice for classic deli sandwiches.

Put the yeast and water into the bowl of a standard electric mixer fitted with a dough hook, or into a large mixing bowl if making by hand, and stir for 1–2 minutes, or until dissolved. Stir in the sugar, oil, half the rye flour, and 5 oz/140 g of the all-purpose flour and beat until just combined. Cover with a dish towel and leave to rise in a warm place for 10 minutes, or until the mixture looks puffed and begins to foam.

Beat in the salt, caraway seeds, and the remaining rye flour and beat until combined. Gradually beat in the remaining flour on slow speed, or mix by hand, until well blended and a firm dough forms. Beat until the dough becomes smooth and elastic, adding more all-purpose flour if necessary.

Turn the dough out on to a floured work surface and knead for 7–10 minutes, working in as much more flour as the dough will absorb. Lightly oil a large bowl and add the dough, turning to coat completely to prevent a crust from forming. Cover with the dish towel and leave to rise in a warm place for 1½–3 hours, or until doubled in volume.

Grease a large baking sheet. Turn the dough out on to a lightly floured surface and knead lightly to deflate. Divide the dough in half and shape each half into a ball, then elongate to an oval about 6 × 4 inches/ 15 × 10 cm. Transfer to the baking sheet. Cover with the dish towel and leave to rise in a warm place for 45 minutes, or until risen.

Meanwhile, preheat the oven to 400°F/200°C. Brush each loaf with beaten egg and sprinkle with caraway seeds. Bake for 35 minutes, or until sounding hollow when tapped on the bottom. Cool on a wire rack. Serve with a variety of fillings, such as pastrami and gherkins.

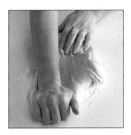

kubaneh

serves 8

40 minutes, plus 3 hours 45
minutes standing and proving

1 hour 15 minutes–
1 hour 30 minutes

1 tbsp easy-blend dried yeast
6 tbsp sugar
1/2 cup warm water
3 1/2 cups all-purpose flour, plus extra
    if necessary and for dusting
1 tsp salt

1/2 tsp ground ginger
4 oz/115 g butter or margarine,
    softened
1 3/4 cups boiling water
vegetable oil, for oiling

*Kubaneh is a sweet Yemenite
Sabbath breakfast bread. Since the
Yemenites arrived in Israel, they
have had access to cheap sugar
and the original slightly sweetened
bread has become much sweeter.*

cook's tip

*If you like, you can carefully
remove the foil, allowing the steam
to escape, and bake for a further
15 minutes, or until the bread is
golden-brown. This soft, slightly
steamed bread is delicious served
warm with conserves or a slightly
spicy chutney or salsa.*

Put the yeast, 1 teaspoon of the sugar and the warm water into the bowl of a standard electric mixer fitted with a dough hook, or into a large mixing bowl if making by hand, and stir for 1–2 minutes, or until dissolved. Sprinkle over a little of the flour and cover with a dish towel. Leave to rise in a warm place for 5–7 minutes, or until the mixture begins to bubble.

In a separate large mixing bowl, combine the remaining sugar, flour, salt, ginger, and half the butter, and beat in the boiling water. Continue beating until the sugar is dissolved, the butter is melted, and the mixture is blended. Add to the yeast mixture and beat on low speed, or mix by hand, until a soft dough forms, adding a little more flour if necessary. Knead on medium speed for 5–7 minutes, or by hand for 15 minutes, or until soft and smooth.

Oil a large bowl and add the dough, turning to coat completely to prevent a crust forming. Cover with the dish towel and leave to rise in a warm place for 1 1/2–2 hours, or until doubled in volume.

Turn the dough out on to a lightly floured work surface and knead lightly to deflate. Return the dough to the bowl, re-cover and leave to rise in a warm place for 1 hour. Preheat the oven to 325°F/160°C. Coat a 10-inch/25-cm ring pan with half the remaining butter and heavily grease a sheet of foil the same diameter as the pan.

Turn the dough out on to a lightly floured work surface. Knead to deflate. Divide into 8 equal pieces, rolling each into a ball. Place the balls in the pan, just touching each other. Cover and leave to rise for 30 minutes, or until the balls are puffed and risen and forming a ring. Dot the remaining butter over the top. Cover tightly with the foil. Bake for 1 1/4–1 1/2 hours, or until the bread pulls away from the pan side. Invert on to a wire rack to cool.

cinnamon
raisin schnecken

makes 24 pastries

**30 minutes, plus 2 hours
45 minutes proving**

15–18 minutes

dough

3½ cups strong bread flour, plus
   extra for dusting

1 tsp salt

3 tbsp sugar

1 tsp easy-blend dried yeast

3 tbsp white vegetable fat, diced

1 egg, lightly beaten

½ cup warm milk

½ cup warm water

filling

½ cup sugar

4 tbsp soft light brown sugar

1 tsp ground cinnamon

3 oz/85 g butter, softened, plus extra
   for greasing

2 oz/55g raisins or golden raisins

½ cup chopped walnuts
   or pecan nuts

*These coiled, cinnamon-scented
pastries are called schnecken, or
"snail" in German, because of their
shape. Brought to the US and
Britain by German Jews who
enjoyed them with coffee, they
remain firm favorites.*

cook's tip

*Baking them in muffin cups or
deep bun tins helps keep the
schnecken from unwinding. If
baked in a heavily greased cake
pan, they join together to make a
coffeecake with soft pastry rounds
which can be pulled apart.*

Sift the flour, salt, and sugar into a medium bowl and stir in the yeast. Stir in the fat and make a well in the center. Beat the egg, milk, and water together in a separate bowl until well blended. Add to the well and stir into the flour mixture until a soft dough forms. Turn out on to a lightly floured work surface. Knead for 5–7 minutes, or until smooth and elastic.

Oil a large bowl, add the dough and turn to coat to prevent a crust forming. Cover with a dish towel. Leave to rise in a warm place for 1½–2 hours, or until doubled in size. Turn out and knead lightly to deflate. Prepare the filling. Combine the sugars and cinnamon in a small bowl.

Generously grease 2 x 12-cup muffin or bun pans. Roll the dough into a large rectangle slightly less than ¼ inch/5 mm thick. Cut vertically in half. Spread the butter over both dough pieces. Sprinkle the sugar mixture evenly over the dough, then sprinkle with the fruit and nuts.

Starting at one long side, tightly roll each piece into a long loaf shape. Lay seam-side down. Cut into 1-inch/2.5-cm slices in one downward movement. Arrange each spiral in a muffin or bun pan. Cover with the dish towel and leave to rise again in a warm place for 30–45 minutes. Preheat the oven to 400°F/200°C. Bake for 15–18 minutes, or until puffed and golden. Remove to a wire rack to cool. Serve warm.

date & nut bread

makes about 12 slices 🍴

**20 minutes,
plus 5 minutes standing** 🥄

1 hour 🕐

1 ¼ cups self-rising flour, plus extra
   for dusting
¼ tsp salt
½–1 tsp ground ginger
1 ⅓ cups chopped dried dates
1 tsp bicarbonate of soda

⅔ cup boiling water
1 egg, lightly beaten
1 tbsp butter or margarine, softened
1 cup chopped walnuts, pecans
   or almonds

*In biblical times, a bountiful
harvest of dates and figs was a
sign of good luck for the coming
years. Centuries later, Ashkenazic
Jews living in harsh climates
depended on dried fruit for
vitamins and minerals and to
enliven an otherwise bland diet.*

cook's tip

*This bread is particularly good
served with goat's cheese or
spread with cream cheese.*

Preheat the oven to 325°F/160°C. Grease a 8 x 4-inch/20 x 10-cm loaf
pan. Line the base and sides with nonstick baking parchment to come
about 1 inch/2.5 cm above the sides. Grease again and dust with flour. Sift
the flour, salt, and ginger into a bowl.

Put the dates into a large bowl with the bicarbonate of soda. Pour over
the boiling water and leave to stand for 5 minutes.

Stir the egg and butter, and flour mixture into the date mixture and beat
with a wooden spoon until well blended. Stir in the nuts. Pour the mixture
into the pan, smoothing the top. Tap the pan gently on a surface to expel
any air bubbles.

Bake in the center of the oven for 1 hour, or until set and well colored and
the bread begins to pull away from the sides of the pan; a knife inserted
in the center should come out clean.

Transfer to a wire rack to cool for 5 minutes, then leave to cool
completely. Using the paper as a guide, carefully remove the bread from
the pan. If not serving the same day, keep in the paper to prevent drying
out. To serve, remove the paper from the base and sides and thinly slice.

poppy seed & prune plait

serves 12–14

40 minutes, plus 3 hours 15
minutes standing and proving

30 minutes

I tbsp easy-blend dried yeast
4 tbsp sugar
4 tbsp warm water
½ tsp salt
4 tbsp warm milk
4 tbsp unsalted butter, softened, plus
  extra for greasing
I egg, lightly beaten, plus I egg
  beaten with I tbsp milk, for glazing
3¼ cups all-purpose flour, plus extra
  if necessary and for dusting

filling
I½ cups poppy seeds
4 tbsp sugar
¾ cup pitted prunes, chopped
grated zest and juice of I orange
4 tbsp sour cream
I tbsp honey
½–I tsp ground cinnamon
2 cups confectioners' sugar

*One of the great traditions of
German, Austrian, and Hungarian
Jews who emigrated to the US and
Britain was the kaffeeklatsch, an
informal gathering for morning
coffee and conversation, at which
many cakes, pastries, and fruit-filled
breads such as this were served.*

Put the yeast and sugar into the bowl of a standard electric mixer fitted
with a dough hook. Stir in the water. Cover with a dish towel and leave to
stand for 5–7 minutes, or until it begins to bubble. Beat in the salt, milk,
butter, and egg until well blended. Beat in the flour on low speed until a
soft dough forms, adding more flour if the dough is sticky. Beat on medium
speed for 2 minutes, or until the dough is smooth and elastic. Turn out on
to a floured work surface. Knead for 2–3 minutes, adding more flour if
necessary. Oil a large bowl and add the dough, turning to coat. Cover and
leave to rise in a warm place for 1½–2 hours, or until doubled in volume.

Put all the filling ingredients, except the orange juice and confectioners'
sugar, into a food processor. Pulse until blended but not completely smooth.

Turn the dough out on to a lightly floured work surface and knead lightly
to deflate. Roll out into a 15 × 10-inch/ 38 × 25-cm rectangle. Transfer to
a greased baking sheet. Spread filling down the center third. Cut 8–10
diagonal slashes ¾ inch/2 cm from either side of the filling to the dough
edges. Fold over alternate strips from each side, tucking the ends under
the plait. Cover and leave to rise in a warm place for 1 hour, or until
doubled in volume. Preheat the oven to 375°F/ 190°C. Brush the plait with
egg. Bake for 30 minutes, or until well browned. Cool on a wire rack. Sift
the confectioners' sugar into a small bowl. Whisk in the orange juice until a
smooth glaze forms. Drizzle over the plait.

onion board—pletzel

serves about 20

25 minutes, plus 1 hour
30 minutes–2 hours proving

25–30 minutes

dough

1 tbsp easy-blend dried yeast

3½ cups all-purpose flour, plus extra
  if necessary and for dusting

1 tbsp sugar

1 tsp salt

1 cup hot water

1 tbsp vegetable oil, plus extra for
  greasing

2 large eggs, lightly beaten

filling

2 tbsp vegetable oil

3 onions, finely chopped

salt and pepper

2 tbsp poppy seeds

*The Yiddish word pletzel means
something flat. This flat yeast
dough is smothered with onions,
sprinkled with poppy seeds, and
baked until crisp and golden—it
could almost be called Jewish
focaccia!*

Stir the yeast, flour, sugar, and salt together in the bowl of a standard
electric mixer fitted with a dough hook and make a well in the center. Add
the water, oil, and eggs and beat on low speed for 2 minutes, or until
combined. Continue beating on medium speed for 5 minutes, or until the
dough is smooth and elastic and leaves the side of the bowl. Cover with a
dish towel and leave in a warm place for 1½–2 hours, or until doubled in
volume. Turn the dough out on to a lightly floured work surface and knead
for 2–3 minutes to deflate, adding a little more flour if the dough is sticky.

Prepare the filling. Heat the oil in a large skillet over medium heat. Add the
onions and cook for 5 minutes, or until softened, stirring frequently. Season
to taste with salt and pepper. Remove from the heat.

Preheat the oven to 375°F/190°C. Grease a large baking sheet. Turn the
dough out on to a lightly floured work surface and knead lightly to deflate.
Roll out a 12 x 10-inch/30 x 25-cm rectangle.

Transfer to the baking sheet. Using your fingertips, push the dough from
the center towards the edges until the rectangle measures about
16 x 14 inches/40 x 35 cm. Crimp the edges to make a raised edge and
press the surface lightly with your thumb to make indentations. Spread the
onion mixture over the surface and sprinkle with poppy seeds. Bake on the
lower shelf of the oven for 20–25 minutes, or until lightly golden and the
base is crisp and brown. Cool on a wire rack. Cut into squares or rectangles.

sufganiyot

makes 24 doughnuts

35 minutes, plus 1 hour
30 minutes–2 hours proving

35–40 minutes

1 tbsp easy-blend dried yeast

3½ cups all-purpose flour, plus extra
for dusting

¼ tsp salt

2 tbsp sugar, plus extra for rolling

1¼ cups warm milk

4 egg yolks

3 tbsp very soft butter, sour cream
or vegetable oil

vegetable oil, for frying

plum, apricot, red currant,
or black currant jelly

½ cup sugar

*Sufganiyot are jelly-filled doughnuts
eaten in Israel at the festival of
Hanukkah. Sweet fritters fried in
oil and soaked in syrup have been
part of the Sephardic tradition for
centuries, probably descended from
the Greek loukomades.*

Stir the yeast, flour, salt, and sugar together in the bowl of a standard electric mixer fitted with a dough hook. Make a well in the center. Add the milk, egg yolks, and butter. Beat on low speed for 2 minutes, or until combined. Beat on medium speed for 5 minutes, or until the dough is smooth and elastic and leaves the side of the bowl. Cover with a dish towel and leave in a warm place for 1½–2 hours, until doubled in volume.

Turn the dough out onto a lightly floured work surface and knead lightly to deflate, adding a little more flour if the dough is sticky. Divide the dough in half and roll out each piece to ¾ inch/2 cm thick.

Working with one dough half at a time, using a 2-inch/5-cm cutter, stamp out as many rounds as possible. Knead the scraps together, re-roll and stamp out more rounds; you should have at least 24. Cover with the dish towel and leave for 20 minutes, or until puffed and slightly risen.

Heat at least 3 inches/7.5 cm of oil in a deep-fat fryer, wok or large pan to 350–375°F/180–190°C, or until a cube of bread browns in 30 seconds. Working in batches, fry the doughnuts, covered, for 3–4 minutes, or until golden. Turn and fry for 3 minutes, or until well colored. Using a skimmer or slotted spoon, transfer to paper towels to drain.

Fit a small pastry bag with a ½-inch/1-cm plain tip and fill with jelly. Put the sugar into a bowl. As the doughnuts are cool enough to handle, make a small slit in the side of each, insert the tip into the center and squeeze in about 1 teaspoon of the jelly. Drop each filled doughnut into the sugar and turn to coat completely. Transfer to a wire rack.

apple strudel

serves 4–6

30 minutes

25 minutes

filling

2 large dessert apples

4 tbsp sugar

1/2 cup raisins or golden raisins

2 tbsp chopped walnuts, pecans or almonds

I tsp ground cinnamon or ginger

grated zest of I small lemon, plus I tbsp of the juice

4 sheets phyllo pastry, thawed if frozen

4 oz/115 g unsalted butter or pareve margarine, melted, plus extra for greasing

1/2 cup fine dry breadcrumbs, matzo meal or ground almonds

confectioners' sugar, for dusting

The Sephardic Jews have used phyllo for centuries. It probably reached Hungary with the Turkish invasion and it was the Hungarian bakers who became masters of this pastry. When it reached the coffee houses of Vienna and Budapest, it became known as strudel.

Preheat the oven to 375°F/190°C. Lightly grease a baking sheet. Peel and core the apples, then thinly slice and put into a large bowl. Add the sugar, raisins or golden raisins, nuts, cinnamon, and lemon zest and juice. Toss well to combine.

Unfold the phyllo pastry and lay I sheet on a work surface (if small, join 2 together to make a larger sheet). Using a pastry brush, brush lightly with melted butter. Sprinkle with about 2 tablespoons of the breadcrumbs. Lay a second sheet of phyllo over the first, brush with butter and sprinkle with 2 more tablespoons of breadcrumbs.

Spoon half the apple mixture along one long end of the phyllo layers, about I inch/2.5 cm from the longer edge and the short edges. Starting with the long end, lift the border over the filling and roll like a jelly roll to enclose the filling. Transfer to one side of the baking sheet, seam-side down.

Repeat, layering the 2 remaining sheets of phyllo with butter, breadcrumbs, and filling with the remaining apple mixture. Transfer to the baking sheet seam-side down. Brush each roll with the remaining butter.

Bake for 25 minutes, or until crisp and golden. Using a long palette knife, transfer each roll to a wire rack to cool for 5 minutes. Dust generously with confectioners' sugar and serve warm.

baklava

makes about 30 diamonds

25 minutes

50 minutes

2 cups pistachios, shelled and skinned

2 tbsp sugar

1/2–1 tsp ground cinnamon

2 tsp rosewater or orange flowerwater

2 oz/55 g butter or pareve margarine, melted, plus extra for greasing

3 1/2 tbsp vegetable oil

10 oz/280 g phyllo pastry, thawed if frozen

syrup

generous 1 cup sugar

4 tbsp honey

3/4 cup water

juice of 1 lemon

2 tsp rosewater or orange flowerwater

Just as Ashkenazic Jews make strudels with apples and raisins to symbolize the harvest and abundance at Sukkoth, the Sephardic Jews of the Middle East layer sheets of phyllo pastry with ground nuts and spices and soak in a rich sugar or honey syrup.

cook's tip

Cutting the layers of pastry and nuts before cooking makes for much easier serving. If you have a choice, use the thinnest phyllo pastry sheets you can find.

Preheat the oven to 350°F/180°C. Grease a shallow baking pan or jelly roll pan about 12 × 8 × 1 inches/30 × 20 × 2.5 cm. Put the nuts into a food processor and process until finely ground, but with some texture remaining. Stir in the sugar, cinnamon, and rosewater.

Combine the melted butter and oil in a small bowl. Depending on their size, cut the sheets of phyllo pastry in half, or trim to fit the baking pan. Brush the pan with a little butter mixture. Lay the first sheet of phyllo on to the base. Brush with a little butter mixture and cover with another sheet. Continue in the same way, using about half the pastry. Spread the nut mixture evenly over the phyllo layers, then continue to layer the remaining phyllo sheets, brushing with the butter mixture between each sheet.

Using a sharp knife, carefully cut vertical lines right though the pastry-nut layers about 1 1/2 /4 cm inches apart. Cut diagonal lines the other way to form small diamond shapes. Bake for 20 minutes in the center of the oven.

Reduce the oven temperature to 300°F/150°C. Bake for 20 minutes more. Transfer to a wire rack to cool for 10 minutes. Meanwhile, prepare the syrup. Put the sugar, honey, and water into a small pan. Bring to a boil, swirling to dissolve the sugar, and boil for 6 minutes. Stir in the lemon juice and rosewater. Leave to cool slightly. Slowly pour the syrup over the baklava. Leave to cool completely and until the syrup is absorbed. Store, covered, in a cool place. Serve at room temperature.

french pear and
almond tart

pastry

1½ cups all-purpose flour, plus extra
for dusting

½ tsp salt

4 tbsp confectioners' sugar

4 oz/115 g unsalted margarine or
butter, diced, plus extra for
greasing

2 egg yolks, beaten with 1 tbsp ice-
cold water

filling

2 eggs, separated

4 tbsp sugar

1 cup ground almonds

½ tsp almond extract

2 large dessert pears, peeled, cored,
and sliced

2 tbsp slivered almonds, for
sprinkling (optional)

*Fresh baked tarts and pastries are
a favorite among French Jews
because they look stunning, often
contain fresh fruit and, if made
with margarine, do not contain
dairy products.*

cook's tip

*This tart has a rich pastry which
can be difficult to handle, but it is
so delicious that it is worth trying.
Keep the ingredients cold; if the
pastry becomes too soft, return it
to the refrigerator to firm up.*

Prepare the pastry. Put the flour, salt, and sugar into a food processor and
pulse to blend. Scatter the margarine over the flour and process until fine
crumbs form. Add the egg mixture and process until a dough begins to
form; do not allow the dough to form a ball or it will be tough. Turn out
on to a floured work surface. Knead 3–4 times to blend. Shape into a ball,
flatten to a disk shape and refrigerate for 2–3 hours or overnight.

Lightly grease a 9–10-inch/23–25-cm loose-bottom flan pan. Roll out the
dough on a lightly floured work surface to a round about ¼ inch/5 mm
thick. Use to line the pan, rolling the rolling pin over the edge to trim the
excess pastry. Prick the base with a fork. Crimp the edge. Refrigerate,
covered, for least 1 hour. Preheat the oven to 400°F/200°C.

Line the pastry with a circle of foil or nonstick baking parchment and fill
with beans. Bake in the center of the oven for 10–15 minutes. Meanwhile,
prepare the filling. Beat the egg yolks and sugar with an electric mixer for
3–4 minutes, or until pale and thick. Beat in the ground almonds and
almond extract. In a separate bowl, beat the egg whites with cleaned
beaters until stiff peaks form. Fold the whites into the yolk mixture.

Transfer the tart to a wire rack and remove paper and beans. Arrange the
pear slices on the base, overlapping. Spoon the almond mixture over the
top. Sprinkle with slivered almonds, if using. Bake for 15–18 minutes, or
until puffed and golden.

rum-soaked babka

serves 8

20 minutes, plus 2–2 hours
30 minutes soaking & proving

30–40 minutes

1 tbsp easy-blend dried yeast
2¹/2 cups all-purpose flour
4 tbsp sugar
¹/4 tsp salt
²/3 cup warm milk
3 eggs, lightly beaten
4 tbsp unsalted butter or margarine, softened, plus extra for greasing
1 tsp vanilla extract
1 tsp rum extract (optional)
¹/2 cup chopped walnuts, pecans, hazelnuts or almonds

¹/2 cup raisins or golden raisins, soaked in water for 10 minutes and drained
¹/4 cup chopped candied orange or lemon peel
slivered almonds, for sprinkling

rum syrup
¹/2 cup sugar
¹/2 cup water
2 tbsp rum or 2 tsp rum extract

Babka is an egg- and butter-rich yeast dough of Russian-Polish origins. It has a more open texture than brioche and is usually studded with dried fruit, nuts, and candied peel.

Stir the yeast, flour, sugar, and salt together in the bowl of a standard electric mixer fitted with a dough hook. Make a well in the center. Add the milk and beat on low speed to combine. Gradually beat in the eggs, butter, and vanilla and rum essences for 2 minutes, or until a soft, smooth batter forms (the batter is very soft and spongy, not like a firm bread dough). Cover the bowl with a dish towel and leave to rise in a warm place for 1–1¹/2 hours, or until almost doubled in volume.

Generously grease a 9- or 10-inch/23- or 25-cm kugelhopf pan, fluted cake pan or ring pan. Add the nuts, raisins or golden raisins, and peel to the dough. Beat on low speed to blend. Sprinkle the pan base with slivered almonds. Scrape the dough into the pan and tap gently to distribute evenly. Cover and leave to rise in a warm place for 45 minutes, or until it almost reaches the pan top. Meanwhile, preheat the oven to 350°F/180°C. Bake for 30–40 minutes, or until puffed, golden, and firm when pressed with a fingertip. Remove to a wire rack and pierce the surface all over with a skewer.

Bring the sugar and water to a boil in a small pan, swirling to dissolve the sugar. Boil for 3 minutes. Remove from the heat. Stir in the rum. Drizzle over the hot cake. Leave to stand until the syrup is absorbed.

israeli olive rolls

makes 16 rolls

30 minutes, plus
2 hours 15 minutes proving

20–25 minutes

1 tbsp easy-blend dried yeast
3/4 cup buckwheat flour, plus extra
  for dusting
2²/3 cups all-purpose flour
1 tsp sugar
1/2 tsp salt

pepper
1 cup warm water
2–3 tbsp extra virgin olive oil
3 cups black olives in brine, drained,
  pitted, and chopped

*Olives and their oil have been an
important part of Jewish history
and food. Olive oil was used in the
temples for ceremonial offerings,
anointing, and in lamps. At the
festival of Hanukkah, it was used
for frying foods to commemorate
the miracle of the oil.*

Stir the yeast, flours, sugar, salt, and pepper to taste together in the bowl
of a standard electric mixer fitted with a dough hook. Make a well in the
center. Add the water and oil and beat on low speed to combine.

Continue beating on medium speed, gradually scattering in the olives, and
knead for 4 minutes, or until a soft smooth dough forms. Cover with a dish
towel and leave to rise in a warm place for 1–1½ hours, or until doubled
in volume.

Turn the dough out on to a lightly floured work surface and knead lightly
to deflate. Shape into a ball and cut into 4 pieces. Roll each piece into a
ball and cut into 4 pieces again to make 16 equal-sized pieces.

Lightly grease 2 large baking sheets. Working with floured hands, shape
each dough piece into a ball or an elongated oval shape and arrange them
on the baking sheets. Cover with the dish towel and leave to rise in a
warm place for 30–40 minutes, or until almost doubled in size. Meanwhile,
preheat the oven to 400°F/200°C.

Dust the rolls very lightly with the extra buckwheat flour (the easiest way
is to use a small strainer). Use a sharp knife to make 2 slashes, or an "X,"
on the top of each roll and bake on the lowest oven shelf for 20–25
minutes, or until crisp and browned and sounding hollow when tapped on
the base. Remove to a wire rack to cool for 2 minutes, then turn out on
to the rack to cool. Serve warm or at room temperature.

zwetschgenkuchen

serves 6–8

**45 minutes,
plus 45 minutes chilling**

40–50 minutes

pastry

grated zest of 1 lemon

4 tbsp superfine sugar

1¼ cups all-purpose flour

4 oz/115 g unsalted butter, chilled, diced

1 large or 2 small egg yolks, beaten with 1 tbsp brandy (optional)

filling

2 tbsp good-quality plum conserve

1 tbsp brandy or water

2 lb 4 oz/1 kg black plums, preferably Swetschgen, washed, quartered and pitted

5 tbsp sugar

1 tsp ground cinnamon

freshly grated nutmeg, to taste

This German-Jewish tart is usually prepared around the time of Rosh Hashanah (New Year) when plums are coming into season. Do not use very juicy plums or the pastry will be soggy, but apricots work well. The pastry is a melt-in-the-mouth crust, flavored with brandy.

Prepare the pastry. Grease a 9–10-inch/23–25-cm loose-bottom flan case. Put half the lemon zest and sugar into a food processor and process until the sugar is a lemony color. Add the flour and process to blend. Add the butter and process for 20–30 seconds, or until fine crumbs form. Pour the egg mixture evenly over the flour mixture and process for 20–30 seconds more, or until a ball begins to form. Turn out on to a lightly floured work surface. Knead lightly to blend. Shape into a ball and flatten to a 1-inch/2.5-cm thick disk. Refrigerate, tightly wrapped, for 30 minutes.

Turn the dough out on to a large sheet of plastic wrap or nonstick baking parchment. Cover with another piece the same size. Starting from the center and working outward, carefully roll the dough into a circle about ¼ inch/5 mm thick. Peel off the top layer and gently ease the pastry into the pan.

Peel off the bottom layer and press the pastry into the base of the pan, making a neat edge. Trim any excess and prick the bottom with a fork. (If the pastry becomes too soft to work with, slide it on to a baking sheet and chill until easier to handle.) Refrigerate for 15 minutes. Meanwhile, preheat the oven to 375°F/190°C.

Prepare the filling. Stir the plum conserve and brandy together and spread evenly over the pastry. Arrange the plum quarters in concentric circles, overlapping if necessary. Combine the sugar, cinnamon, nutmeg, and remaining lemon rind and sprinkle evenly over the plums. Bake in the center of the oven for 40–50 minutes, or until the pastry is golden and the plums are bubbling.

moroccan cigares

makes about 50 cookies

40 minutes, plus 1 hour thawing

30–40 minutes

25 frozen egg-roll skins (won ton skins), thawed for 1 hour
vegetable oil, for deep-frying
4 tbsp good-quality honey
½ cup water

filling
3½ cups blanched almonds
2½ cups sugar
1 small egg, lightly beaten
1 tbsp rosewater or orange flowerwater, plus extra for sprinkling (optional)
grated zest of 1 small lemon

These delicate cigar-shaped cookies are traditionally made with phyllo pastry, but using frozen egg-roll skins is a handy trick! This type of sweetmeat is eaten all over the Middle East. They are a little sticky, but perfect with an espresso or Greek coffee after dinner.

cook's tip

If egg-roll skins are unavailable, use spring-roll skins instead.

Prepare the filling. Put the almonds and half the sugar in a food processor and process until finely ground, but with some texture remaining. Add the remaining sugar, egg, rosewater, and lemon zest. Set aside.

Lay the egg-roll skins on a work surface and cut crosswise in half to make 50 pieces. Place 1 teaspoon of the filling along the edge of a skin and fold over the pastry. Brush the opposite side with a little water to moisten, then fold the 2 open ends over to enclose the filling. Roll up like a jelly roll to make a cigar. Place seam-side down on a large baking sheet (or 2). Continue rolling and filling.

Heat 4 inches/10 cm of oil in a deep-fat fryer, large deep pan or wok to 350–375°F/180–190°C, or until a cube of bread browns in 30 seconds. Working in batches, fry the "cigars" for 2–3 minutes, or until crisp and golden, turning occasionally. Remove to paper towels to drain.

Bring the honey and water to a boil in a small pan over high heat. Reduce the heat and simmer for 5 minutes. Remove from the heat and leave to cool slightly.

Using kitchen tongs, dip each "cigar" into the syrup, turning to coat. Transfer to a wire rack to cool, then arrange on a serving dish. Sprinkle with a little more rosewater, if you like.